Natural Healing
Quiet & Calm

Helene Finizio

Kusal Goonewardena

Helene Finizio operates a private practice in executive life coaching called LoveLight Consulting. She specializes in meditation and positive psychology to help her clients clear their minds decrease stress increase productivity and efficiency and overall feelings of wellbeing.

Kusal Goonewardena is an elite athlete sports physiotherapist. Kusal is the founder of sports medicine clinics in Australia, and mentor to thousands of physiotherapy students from around the world. For more information you can visit: www.eliteakademy.com/whos-kusal

Published by:
Wilkinson Publishing Pty Ltd
ACN 006 042 173
Level 4, 2 Collins St Melbourne, Victoria, Australia 3000
Ph: +61 3 9654 5446
www.wilkinsonpublishing.com.au

International distribution by Pineapple Media Limited
(www.pineapple-media.com)   ISSN 2203-0840

National Library of Australia Cataloguing-in-Publication data:

Creator:	Finizio, Helene, author.
Title:	Natural healing : quiet & calm / Helene Finizio & Kusal Goonewardena.
ISBN:	9781925265583 (paperback)
Subjects:	Meditation. Mind and body. Cooking (Natural foods) Healing.
Other Creators/Contributors:	Goonewardena, Kusal, author.
Dewey Number:	158.12
Layout Design:	Tango Media Pty Ltd
Cover Design:	Tango Media Pty Ltd

Photos by agreement with iStock.

Table of Contents

CHAPTER 1

THE CHALLENGES OF EVERYDAY LIFE

You might be one amongst the millions who spends a lot of time working on goals for the future. Goals are equivalent to objects, targets, results, achievements, resolutions, aims, ambitions, and other things you want to attain. Leading a quality life, however, has become scarce. The fast pace of life and the increasing pressure to create an identity in the world are pushing your "real" life down.

The growing consent to be unique among the increasing population is leading to stress and depression that affects the individual's personality. A person develops fear, which becomes the biggest hurdle to overcome. Succeeding in overcoming that fear is the imperative element for a person to able to perform his or her role in the world.

What is the negativity bias? In simple terms it is our tendency to focus on the negative. Our bias towards looking at what is going wrong, rather than what is going right. Our cultural norms tend to speak to a connection with other people being based on what is *not* working or what is problematic. Most jobs are based on Fixing Problems. Most of western medicine is focused on Treatment as opposed to Prevention. We, as a global culture, are often inundated with news stories about everything that is going wrong, rather than everything that is going right.

Our negativity bias can be dated back to our ancient DNA, when our ancestors were told to be ever vigilant of the sabre-toothed cat that may be lurking around any corner, ready to pounce and eat us at any given moment. This was a constant state of fight-or-flight vigilance on the molecular level, a constant state of hyper vigilance present to ensure our cellular survival! If we were always ready for the worst, we just may be able to survive another day.

Our brains have been set up to support these systems of life preservation, and those neural pathways have been passed down from generation to generation. The nature of the brain is such that we build up channels and connections from one neuron to the next as we think and act in accordance with what seems to be best in any given moment. Given that survival is one of the strongest instincts in the human condition, those actions that ensured our survival were engrained so deeply and with such gusto that the concerns about those old sabre-toothed cats have still left an imprint in our brains today. So on the physical level, our bodies and brains want us to be aware of problems in order to protect against death.

What this means is that our central nervous system tends to support fixing problems as a very gratifying experience. It releases high amounts of endorphins and "happy hormones" such as dopamine, serotonin and norepinephrine when we protect ourselves against concerns or fix something that isn't working, even if it's as simple as a broken toilet or gate lock.

On the social level, this tendency to look out for the worst has spilled over into how we connect. A research study looked at the types of conversations employees usually had while taking a break and connecting over the water cooler. It found that the predominant types of conversations were negative in focus, and that most people were finding connections with one another based on what was going wrong, rather than uniting over victories and sharing about what was going right! It seems that most people feel much more comfortable sharing the problems in their lives as a source of social interaction and connection. In fact, some people have even reported feeling embarrassed and self-conscious about sharing their victories and successes with peers, with a real concern being they would be viewed as egotistical and braggarts.

What has happened in our social norms that we have somehow set up a standard of complaint over gratitude? Where have we lost our way, so that the terrible events of the world gain infinitely more attention than the blessings and goodness of humanity, as well as the miracles that happen every day? Why have we spent so many more dollars on war and acts of violence than acts of education, unification and peace?

There is evidence supporting a 3:1 ratio of negative thoughts to positive thoughts, and this is pervasive in many countries all over the world. This means that for every one positive thought we tend to have three negative thoughts. In the cognitive neuroscience research studies looking at the general activity of the brain, we see about 70,000 thoughts running through an adult human brain Every Single Day. 70,000!!! That means that the 3:1 ratio has an extraordinary spread, with tens of thousands of negative thoughts dominating over positive thoughts in our internal dialogue each and every day. In response to this, the field of Positive Psychology has been looking at the nature of positive experience, strengths and what is going Right in the human experience. This is also a response to the focus on the negative in most of psychology and science to date. Researchers in Positive Psychology have found a correlation between shifting negative to positive thoughts ratio from 3:1 to 1:3 and overall well-being and happiness. That means that if we can move from having three negative thoughts for every one positive thought to three positive thoughts for every one positive thought, we can change how we feel on a daily basis. We can increase our own well being and become happier.

POSITIVE PSYCHOLOGY HAS BEEN LOOKING AT THE NATURE OF POSITIVE EXPERIENCE, STRENGTHS AND WHAT IS GOING RIGHT IN THE HUMAN EXPERIENCE.

We have also seen that people who have overall higher ratings of happiness and well-being tend to be healthier, taking less sick days, performing better at work, have greater productivity levels at large and live longer.

Sound good? It does to me too!

So how do we get there? How does someone challenge our DNA, social norms, as well as the pervasive, automatic ticker tape of constant negative thoughts that flows through our brains, and shift that ratio?

1. **Addressing Self-doubt:** We often think that negativity is an unshakable, unchangeable truth of life. Somehow, no matter what we do or who we are, there will be a predominance of negativity in our lives and it is only "realistic" that we accept this as a truth in order to survive life and act like 'an adult.' If being an adult means accepting a constant stream of negative thinking, I'll be with Peter Pan in Neverland. The fact is we DO have the power to change our thinking. We DO have the ability to shift the ratio from 3:1 to 1:3 and become much more positive while at the same time still acknowledging and addressing the negative as needed. No matter how difficult our life circumstances are; no matter how challenging our days can be, we can always choose how we frame our experiences, and how we interact with our lives. We have that choice in each and every moment. It's the beauty and responsibility of free will and it's up to each one of us to choose how we will wield that power and gift in each and every moment.

2. **From Pessimism to Optimism:** One of the greatest combatants against negative thinking is adopting an Optimistic Thinking Style. In order to understand optimism, we might first look at Pessimism. Pessimism is generally described as 'glass half-empty' thinking. If there is a glass of water sitting on a table, and it is filled up only half way, the pessimist will look at the glass and remark, "This glass is half-empty!" and perhaps be upset that it is lacking. This is a perspective of what is not here, what is going wrong, what is the problem and how I can I find a reason to be unhappy about whatever is in front of me. People apply pessimistic thinking styles to just about everything, often unconsciously. "I don't have enough money," "I don't have enough time," "I'm not beautiful/handsome enough," "I'm not enough, period." We can find an infinite number of reasons to choose pessimism, and the results will be consistent; we will find ourselves upset, perhaps even panicked, and likely give ourselves more reasons to feel bad and perhaps even treat ourselves poorly by drinking to excess, procrastinating on an important project, or simply saying extremely harsh things to ourselves, the like of which we would never say to someone else. We are generally harder on ourselves than anyone else ever could or would be, and harder on ourselves than we ever would be to another.

✣ ✣ ✣

Optimism is a choice and a practice. It takes hard work and dedication, and a commitment to living a healthier and happier life for yourself and others. Optimists look at the same glass that is half-filled with water and look at it as half-full. An optimist looks at what is going right, what is present that is of value, what is working and what there is to be grateful for. Optimism rises above DNA-based programming and chooses to consciously interact with the good in the world and sharing that perspective with others. Simply choosing an optimistic thought over

a negative thought can in and of itself be an act of healing. When we share that optimistic thought with another, it can be an act of sharing healing energy. When we choose to feel good, we are opening the door for our own unique gifts to flow, for the goodness in our lives and in our world to be acknowledged and supported, and for those around us to learn by our example and perhaps model our behaviour and help others as well. This is how global healing works. This is how movements begin. It starts exactly where we are with what we've got, and we happen to have a LOT.

THE DIS-EASE MODEL AND THE POSITIVE PSYCHOLOGY RESPONSE:

Most of psychology thus far has been based on the Dis-Ease model. The focus of most of the field has been on what can and may go wrong, what is not working, what hurts, and what is calling a lack of ease, or stress. The general emphasis on the pain points, while perhaps valuable from a business point of view, can leave people stuck in a rut and feeling a sense of hopelessness. When someone is given a label, it can be useful to understand a set of experiences and symptoms, or it can be taxing and cause greater feelings of turmoil and suffering.

Positive Psychology, the psychology of what is Right with you, was founded as a response to this focus in most of psychology on the negative. Martin Seligman and his colleagues began the field just two short decades ago in an effort to support a focus on what is going Right, our Strengths, our natural abilities and all that we are capable of. In Positive Psychology, researchers like Jonathan Haidt speak about something called Post Traumatic Growth, the other side of the PTSD coin. Post Traumatic Growth includes the notion that after going through a trauma, which we have all experienced in our own ways, we actually connect with more of our strengths, our bravery, our awareness and our abilities. We can become richer, fuller individuals for having gone through these experiences and come out the other end.

We are all survivors in our own right. Whether your experience was one of tribal warfare or insensitive parenting, we have all felt pain and had deep emotional responses to our experiences. We are deeply emotional people, whether we want to admit it or not.

The beauty of this truth is that we are fully capable of using our deep emotional experiences to grow, strengthen and become even happier than we ever were before the pain. It is often in the dark where we are able to best see the light.

DEPRESSION, ANXIETY AND STRESS:

In my private practice I work with a lot of very high-powered people. I suppose you could say that I specialize in the 1% of the 1%. Often my clientele are extraordinarily successful in business with tremendous reach in their companies and offerings, and sizable financials.

After going through a very difficult experience in which I had been drugged by a woman I thought I could trust, and set up for some kind of a rape-porn experience, from which I very gratefully escaped, I was diagnosed with something called PTSD, or Post-Traumatic Stress Disorder. This is one of a myriad of disorders available in the DSM-V, the fifth version of the general diagnostic and statistical manual for all the possible problems a person can experience. Now, I don't know about you, but I would imagine that ANYONE, man, woman, adult, child, American, African, whoever, who is drugged and set up for a potentially life-ending or torturous experience would experience a high level of stress after that encounter. In fact, I find that healthy. To have no emotional reaction would have left me numb and disconnected. I faced some very unhealthy people, and I survived, and was immediately labeled with a "disorder." Now, at the time, there was some help in understanding that I was on edge and still hyper-vigilant, and for a short period identifying as someone with PTSD was useful in that way. But over just a short time of talk therapy with a trauma specialist, the label no longer fit and began to feel like a burden and a sentence. Do I still have moments of stress? Of course! Do I ever think about what happened? Absolutely. Do I perhaps read situations with greater critical perspective after having had gone through this? You betcha. I consider this savvy, not problematic.

Somewhere along the way, talk of billions of dollars no longer made me blink and global thinking became the norm. I love working with high-powered folks, and the ability to help grassroots efforts from a place of abundance and tremendous opportunity.

My work in the music and art world has been with many of the 1% of the 1% of the creative culture, with people who are absolutely brilliant at what they do and how they create. Music, art, fashion, performance, these are the currency of many people's lives and fill our world with beauty and passion.

I have also been a volunteer most of my life, working with groups such as at my local church teaching Sunday school for young children, organizations like Food Not Bombs helping to feed the homeless, community development groups such as Burning Man and affiliate groups, and currently the YMCA with many folks who are here to do good in the world and can benefit from some community connection and support.

Across every group I have ever worked with, in all the research I have done in various fields, and in every town I have ever visited, I have noticed the presence of depression, anxiety and stress. Sometimes these presences are larger and sometimes they are smaller. In my experience, there is no demographic that is exempt, no lifestyle that is foolproof, no occupation that 100% prevents one or more of these conditions.

So why is there so much depression, anxiety and stress in our world, across industries, cultures and occupations?

Each of these is a Mindset Manifestation. It is our thoughts and interpretations of input that lead us to feel positive or negative. It is the way in which we interact with our world that leaves us feeling good or bad. We have already discussed our negativity bias and the tendency to focus on problems. Depression, anxiety and stress are the outcomes from this type of thinking style, the result of negativity bias in action.

"We all have the power to shift from depression to enthusiasm and passion, from anxiety to zest, from stress to peacefulness and joy."- Helene

BUT HOW DO WE DO IT? WHAT DOES IT TAKE?

We all have dreams. We plan to reach our dreams one at a time. For this, we plan a schedule and move in that direction. However, if you feel burdened and depressed, due to several reasons, achieving the goal becomes a distant dream. Therefore, learning to overcome fear is an essential criterion.

The challenges faced by any person differ according to their lifestyle and status in the society. The same applies even to educated people who hold high positions in society and the corporate world. Every day is a challenge, and we have to live it successfully. It is possible by planning, concentrating on weaknesses, and seeking professional help.

Of the many challenges that people face, health has become important. We need good health to perform daily activities and achieve our goals without any external and internal stress. It further acts as a foundation to prepare and overcome any challenges that may occur in the future.

However, people often neglect health and only try and redeem themselves after losing precious years. Creating a balanced life is important to achieve your goal without affecting your health. Furthermore, in certain cases you may often feel lost and have no idea to get back on the track.

"DEVELOPING A HEALTHY MINDSET IS THE ANSWER TO OVERCOMING CHALLENGES IN EVERYDAY LIFE."

– KUSAL

In reality, we all struggle in life at some point. The outcome of the struggle depends on how you react to it and whether you choose the solutions in an intelligent way. We have the power to build a strong mindset, which keeps us moving ahead come what may. At the same time, we also possess the ability to lose out and lean towards the negative attitude, which creates trauma. The best example that we can set here is to follow the successful people who created a niche in the world. They have displayed the power and determination that kept them alive even during their worst periods.

Like any other muscle in the human body, overcoming a trouble requires a similar approach to a workout. In fact, exercise plays a prominent role in your life. If you develop that attitude and find solutions to those situations, you will not only master the challenge but also develop confidence that lets you fight against any odds.

KUSAL

The following methods provide you with the opportunity to build a powerful mindset needed to overcome challenges in everyday life.

1. Adversity

Struggling in life builds character. It defines your nature and lets you choose who you want to be in this world. Most often, you feel satisfied when you overcome adversity. They are also the moments that you will cherish for the rest of the life. Learn to work with your limitations rather than blame them. Push the boundaries of your comfort zone and move forward. This will make you unstoppable. Such an attitude strengthens your inner-self and reveals the capabilities that you can accomplish.

2. Team player

Success is not just credited to one person. It is the result of a team. Develop a team with a similar mindset. Find people in the neighborhood, in your college, among your family, or in the workplace. Create a group and drive towards the goal. Group participation increases self-confidence and boosts morale. They will lift you up when you are down.

3. Positive attitude

Every action has two outcomes – positive and negative. Unfortunately, our brain has a natural inclination towards the negative. In order to destroy it and build a positive attitude, move in a world that is full of positive vibrations. Find reasons to appreciate everything around and move with people who are full of energy and positive attitude.

4. Emotions

Learning to label feelings and differentiating them is of utmost importance. When this is done your brain improves logic, focus, and awareness. The next period you find yourself in an emotional situation, differentiate it by labeling it. It will allow you to gain experience and choose the right answer consciously. A simple rule of thumb – a positive emotion will reflect happiness; a negative emotion will result in unhappiness.

5. Your life story

Life itself is a story. Although the brain tends to move towards the negative realm, writing a new story every time is a boost to the morale. If you feel that telling a story has an impact on your performance, it's better to choose one that motivates and empowers. It is in your hands to believe the negativity in a story or create a new one.

6. A journal

Writing a journal when facing a challenge assists in letting out the unconscious brain activity and its thoughts. It will help you in separating from the experience and move towards a logical attitude. It develops focus and awareness that in time improve self-confidence.

7. Exercise

Physical exercises produce a significant impact on the body, mind, and soul. Exercises have a direct bearing on our brain activity. As you would be trying to complete the set goal, you will develop the ability to perform a task with the same attitude. Additionally, with increased blood flow and oxygen, there is radical improvement in brain functionality. Exercises increase brain activity that improves memory skills, grasping power, focus, alertness, and attentive skills.

8. Into the countryside

Experts have revealed that spending time with nature has significant importance in improving overall health. The freshness of the air and the place offers a relaxed environment, which is a critical tool to rejuvenate the body, mind, and soul.

9. Celebrations

Celebrations drive enthusiasm and help you continue to lead the path. Take a moment to celebrate each achievement with friends and family, no matter how small. Pausing and celebrating provides you the boost needed to move ahead with success.

10. New summits

Write down all the goals that you prefer to achieve. It gives you the required focus and emphasizes on drawing out plans. They become the reason to push through any hurdle that might emerge in the journey. People who write down their goals are statistically far more likely to achieve them than those who do not.

Health has become a crucial aspect in every moment of life. When you are at peak of your health, you have a better ability to achieve everything that you dreamt of, and your life journey will be accompanied by much more success and joy.

People residing in the western countries face a series of health diseases. The increase in technology has led to a revolution. However, it equally increased the health ailments. Although technology has allowed us to work faster, cheaper and more accurately, it has come with a price on our health. There is a considerable reduction in physical activity as a result of this shift. It significantly affects health because our exercise levels, metabolic rates and mindset all change. With reduced calorie-burn, they alter to fit and remain in the body, increasing weight

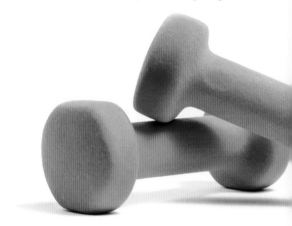

and other health related issues. A person suffering from obesity or excessive weight is prone to heart attack, type II diabetes, cancer causing elements and reduced brain function. Over time, people get lazy, which further reduces locomotion.

The lack of exercise has proven to be the cause of several diseases. Many people who are suffering from diseases have a less active lifestyle. On the other hand, people with an active lifestyle are leading a balanced life comprised of health and happiness. Understanding this will help you move ahead. It also includes achieving your targets and fulfilling your desires.

In general, a human body requires approximately 3000 calories per day for a male and 2500 calories per day for a female. Any excess intake leads to additional calories that turn to fat. You will notice this around the stomach, thighs, and underarms.

Excessive weight leads to obesity, which causes a burden on the skeletal and muscular structures. It even reduces the functionality of the organs. The increased load on the digestive system leads to improper functioning. All these aspects affect the overall operation of the human system. For example, increased fat content reduces the operation of energy development. In turn, it decreases the activeness that humans possess. The co-relation affects the functionality of the system that reduces the blood flow and oxygen supply to several organs and cells in the body. Such a condition provides the opportunity for disease-causing bacteria to infiltrate the body.

Case Study

Jessica, a 55 year old office worker, wanted to lose 20 kg. That's how much weight she had put on since having three children. The children were either adults or in high school now and she wanted to go back to feeling great. With an increase in weight she felt lethargic, joints were hurting, there was osteoarthritis in her knees and her sleep was not great. For two weeks she prepared an exercise diary, planning the next 24 weeks meticulously. She wrote in her book who her exercise buddies were, who would help her professionally – her doctor, physiotherapist and nutritionist and the goals she wanted to achieve. She shared these goals with her children and husband. After planning and mentally preparing herself for the 24 weeks ahead she embarked on her journey of exercise, well being and feeling happy. Some weeks were great and some not so great. But she celebrated each of her mini wins and her team of professionals and her loving family were there to lift her when she was down. She ended up losing 20 kg after 20 weeks. She has no pain in her knees now, feels better than ever before, loves the outdoors again and is the happiest she has been.

CHAPTER 2

HEALTHY BUSY VS. BAD BUSY

So what creates the difference between being busy in a good way, and being busy in a wheel-spinning, "becoming drained with little positive outcome" way?

> "ONE OF THE KEY INGREDIENTS IN FEELING GOOD, DOING GOOD AND CREATING WHAT WE WANT FOR OURSELVES IS A VERY SIMPLE AND VERY POWERFUL THOUGHT STYLE CALLED 'SOLUTION-FOCUSED THINKING.'"
>
> – HELENE

What is Solution-Focused Thinking? It is very much what it sounds like. We often spend a lot of time thinking about what can and could go wrong, or what has gone wrong in the past. This is a symptom of the negativity bias we covered in section 1. Solution-Focused Thinking is the other side of that coin.

Solution-Focused thinking is all about looking for the opportunity in each and every moment. We can spend our lives, our time and our energy thinking about the problems, the downfalls, the difficulties, the strife, and take on a victim mentality. We do have the power to choose to make ourselves miserable, and focusing on the negative is a very effective way to do exactly that. But who wants to be miserable!?

Just as we have the energy and free will available to choose to follow those negative thoughts, we also have that same energy and free will available to follow the positive thoughts! Solution-Focused thinking starts with a choice, and that choice is to Feel Good. We are Choosing to think in a way that aligns us with the actions, behaviours, beliefs and desires that move us more fully in the direction of the future we want for ourselves, even potentially the future we would most Love!

Once we have made the choice to feel good, and to use our thoughts to move us towards a positive outcome, the Art of Solution-Focused Thinking comes into play. How can we, in any moment, in any situation, no matter how bad it may seem, find a way to look at an opportunity to make things just a little bit better, just one step at a time. Sometimes Solution-Focused Thinking can show us a full path all at once, and sometimes it is just one small step. Whatever it is, whatever size, Solution-Focused Thinking is a step Towards Love, Towards Light, Towards Life Feeling Good.

Rosie had just gotten out of a long-term abusive relationship. She was in love with a man who had a lot of charisma, a lot of charm, and a lot of talent, but also had a real dark side and indulged in drugs and alcohol in an addictive pattern. This man had become violent with her and she felt trapped in the relationship and her feelings of love and need for him for years. When she finally left him, it felt like she was learning how to walk again. Nothing in her world made sense. She felt frightened and insecure. But she was willing. She was willing to look at the possibilities of a better life, a better tomorrow, and a better today. She started to ask her close friends for Help. And in these conversations with dear friends, she found advice, guidance and insight that lead her to begin to think about what she was able to change. This is the seed of Solution-Focused Thinking, 'What am I able to do to make things better?' She moved in with someone she trusted, and began, day by day, to create a new life for herself. It wasn't easy, but she took it all one step at a time, and kept asking herself, 'What am I able to do to make things better?' And with this question, and her willingness, and the support of a few close friends, she created a new life filled with goodness, kindness, and personal empowerment.

Now, overall we are talking about being busy in a healthy way. So, what does Solution-Focused Thinking need to partner with to create positive actions and outcomes?

We have all heard the adage, Clarity is Key, and it really is!

Solution-Focused Thinking is only one part. In order to know which solution is optimal given any particular set of circumstances, we need to be able to clearly weigh our options, and clearly understand our current situation. We would also be well served to be able to clearly envision how one set of actions and behaviours might affect our future, even if only a minute or two out.

Clarity is an essential ingredient in a healthy busy lifestyle.

But how does one create more clarity in the past, present and future awareness of one's life and life decisions?

Well, let's consider for a moment very simply what clarity is. Clarity is very simply a lucid understanding of what is, or a freedom from confusion. At its core, clarity is simply the ability to perceive with distinction.

When we show up in our lives, and for ourselves, all we need to do in order to attain some level of clarity is to listen to ourselves, pay attention to what is coming through our sensory experiences, notice the thoughts and beliefs that come up, and allow our honest read on the situation to be heard within ourselves. If fears come up, that's OK. If anxiety comes up, that's alright. Clarity does not mean we exist without emotion. Clarity is about existing With emotion, accepting ourselves fully and allowing our wisdom to show us where we are.

Generally, although this may seem simple enough, clarity can very well be an elusive phenomenon for many.

So what gets in our way?

In working with people from all over the world, all ages and all types of cultural backgrounds, I have seen these three factors get in the way of clarity:

Self-Doubt- second guessing our intuition and awareness

Denial- feeling that the truth simply "could not be real" and fabricating something that 'feels more accurate'

Rushing- when we move so fast and furiously through our lives, we lose the ability to drink in each moment. If we are rushing through our experience, we can lose sight of our own awareness and the voice within which is a dear friend and guide.

Spirituality can come from unexpected places sometimes. I was sitting down with my accountant going over my taxes for this previous year and we were talking about the growth in my business. Profits had gone up by 70%! New opportunities were showing up all the time, the team was growing and we were able to support more product development endeavours to help even more people than ever before. My accountant, we'll call him Peter, was looking at all of this after being a part of business development for years. He looked me right in the eyes and asked me to take a moment, to pause and look at the Spiritual Landscape of what was happening. Ours is a business of mission and purpose First. He helped me to let go of the 'Get It Done' mentality that often accompanies financial matters, like filling taxes, and encouraged me to use the moment to tap into what was happening on

a spiritual level. Kindred people showing up, the vision growing, more resources flowing in to support these efforts, and more doors in the world opening wider to allow this information and energy to flow to more people who could benefit from it. Peter asked me to step back, let go of the rush, step into the now, and feel the good in the present moment. It was only after we took the item to acknowledge this awareness that we completed the task at hand, and it felt more complete having had taken that pause. There are gifts of awareness in every task. It is up to us to show up fully and take note of them. The best teams support one another in taking those pauses where they are needed, and then getting the task at hand completed.

"THERE IS NO NEED TO EVER RUSH ANYTHING, EVER."

– MARCO PELUSI

OK, so we're talking all about what can get in our way, but where is it that we are going? What exactly IS Healthy Busy?

healthy \hel-thē\ *adj.*
the condition of being sound and/or full of vigour

busy \bi-zē\ *adj.* active

So Healthy Busy is being active in our soundness and vigour. It is the state of being in action in a way that supports the flow of our life force energy. Healthy Busy is ultimately about acting in accordance with that which leads us into greater and greater states of well-being, for self and for others.

If Healthy Busy exists, what can we do to be in that state more and more?

Over the years in our private practice, we have seen that people respond much more fully to positive reinforcement than they do negative reinforcement. In fact, there have been studies done to show that positive reinforcement can be up to five times stronger than negative reinforcement, and, if used correctly, can lead to much longer lasting positive outcomes.

So how can this inform the present moment and our goal to step into a Healthy Busy space when desired?

With the incredibly high-achieving people we have worked with, a simple and easy technique has been seen to be effective across the board. We have seen 100% success rates when using this technique. 100%! This is not to say that every possible desired outcome has been achieved. What we have found, though, is that when we use this technique, everyone who has ever used it has seen positive transformation take place in his or her lives. This exercise leaves people better every time. Every. Time.

Ready for us to tell you what it is? We thought so :)

Case Study

Nathaniel owns a business in merchandise sales. He works with multi-billion dollar corporations and services very high-end clientele. He was struggling with work-life balance and time management structures, which go hand in hand. He wanted to work hard, but often found himself feeling unmotivated to get started. We looked at how he was structuring his days, and he found that he really did not have much of a schedule. Every day was different. What we looked at, even though he had a varied schedule, was how at the end of his day he might reward himself for completing a set of needs or tasks. We began looking at small positive reinforcement options, such as taking an hour to watch a funny show, or relaxing with a good meal, or even simply thanking himself for his hard work. When he began to practice these positive reinforcement tools at the end of the day, his motivation went up, his productivity improved, and in this past year he has broken his sales records by over 200%. A little positive reinforcement can go a very, very long way.

Imagine you are writing a goal, and while you are writing you are really connecting with loving energy. You are envisioning what you would most love for yourself, and you are connecting with the flow of loving energy in your life that feels good and right to you beyond the potential doubts that may come up in the 'monkey mind' self-doubt zone. You are connecting with what feels Really Right for You.

This is the essence of this powerhouse exercise: connecting with loving energy while setting goals. It is not right brain vs. left-brain. It is not either pragmatic business sense or passion and zest. It is not making money or following a spiritual path. It is living a full and rich life filled with love and success in harmony.

"THE BEST WAY TO DO IT IS TO DO IT."

– AMELIA EARHART

FUNDAMENTALS TO FITNESS PROGRAMS

Life is what you make and how you live it. The options that you choose and the decisions that you decide, take you on the path of life. You are the sole designer of your future and lead it in the way that you like to be. However, during the course, it is essential to remember that health is of immense importance. You do not want to spend a tremendous amount on hospital bills and medications.

THE LOVE-BASED GOAL STATEMENT TECHNIQUE
FROM HELENE FINIZIO

Step 1 - Breathe

Step 2 - Think about what you would most love

Step 3 - Think about what you would most love to see in the next few hours, days, weeks, months, years

Step 4 - Jot down some notes for each

Step 5 - Underline anything that feels really right for you

Step 6 - Write out the words 'I would love...' 10 times

Step 7 - Fill in the blanks

Step 8 - Review your list and make any additions you would like, either with a new statement or by adding detail to a current statement

Step 9 - Read this list aloud with a colleague, friend, executive coach or trusted advisor

Step 10 - Discuss each one and why it matters

Step 11 - Choose your priorities

Step 12 - Healthy Busy Bonus Step- Match your Daily Actions with your Priority Love-Based Goal Statements

Challenge - We challenge you to try this, even just one statement, and simply watch as positive transformation shows up in your life.

There is an immense difference between being healthy and trying to be healthy. A healthy state includes both a physical and mental presence. Attempting to be healthy is forcing the system to follow an action, which doesn't help the body's performance rather than improving. Humans enjoy their freedom and participate wholeheartedly when they indulge in things that they like to do. In similar way, planning a schedule that works positively helps in sustaining a long healthy and happy lifestyle.

Achieving a healthy state is now possible. Thanks to the availability of technology and groups that assist people with the least active lifestyle. Additionally, they also induce a positive attitude that helps in being healthy even while working. **Learning to keep busy in a healthy way is entirely acceptable.** It enhances productivity at work and reduces the stress that one experiences. Additionally, the entire human system functions to the maximum potential. The improved brain functionality assists in leading a healthy lifestyle with reduced resistance.

> "THE FOLLOWING ARE VARIOUS EXAMPLES THAT HELP YOU TO REMAIN HEALTHY AND OPTIMIZE YOUR EXERCISE TIME RESULTING IN 'HEALTHY BUSY' RATHER THAN 'BAD BUSY'."
>
> **– KUSAL**

A. Physical exercises

Physical exercises have an immense impact on the performance of the brain and internal system. **Exercises help in burning unwanted calories and fat content accumulated within the body.** The stress on the muscular structure improves flexibility and enhances muscle mass. As a result, you will enrich your metabolic rate that in turn increases the calories burnt. A major advantage of the increase in metabolic rate is the ability to burn calories even when the body is idle, such as sleeping.

Physical exercises are available in a number of formats. Each activity concentrates on several muscles of the body and enhances their activeness. However, every action causes a rise in the heart rate. Increased heart rate improves blood pumping, which is an important element to improve the overall functionality. With improved blood flow across the body, every organ, and cells receive the required oxygen. It also promotes the role of the digestive system, which is responsible for energy production.

The body requires energy at frequent intervals of the day. Providing the ability to produce energy at that period becomes possible when you **follow your exercise schedule regularly.**

The exercise program concentrates on improving every part of the body in a systematic manner. The plan includes enjoying different activities every day of the week.

If you are a beginner, it is feasible to consult a physiotherapist, who would assist you in the preparation of the program. Along with the program, they also emphasize on an improved diet control. A well chalked out plan works in an amazing way, and you could start witnessing the results within a few days to a few weeks.

As you work through your program and complete your daily activities you improve not only your health but also your concentration levels, grasping power, problem-solving techniques, and brain activeness.

Majority of the exercises concentrate on cardiovascular activities. Increasing the heart rate is the primary concern, which helps in building a healthy circulation. The best mode of exercise to improve the heart rate is walking. Yes, walking is the simplest form of activity that has an immense effect on overall human system. A walking workout activates most major muscle groups in the body.

Walking comprises variants. These variants are balance, posture, and speed. All three criteria play a crucial role in burning unwanted calories. The 10,000-step program has an immense effect on the daily life. You can turn your dull, least-active lifestyle into an exciting role that fills you with goodness of the life.

The 10,000-step aims at burning unwanted calories in the body using the simplest form of exercise. Walking is the natural locomotion available to people. Regular walking has a positive impact on mind and body. To begin with, the exercise session, you require walking shoes that offer extended support and protection to the lower limb. The second step involves planning the activities that entitle you to complete 10,000 steps in a single day.

These little things count towards the 10,000 steps and help you keep active all through the day.

THE FOLLOWING PROVE THE BENEFITS OF COMPLETE THE TASK:

1. Walking around the house is a good way to begin the day.

2. You may be driving a car to your workplace. Try to park it at least a 15-20 minutes walking distance from your office. Walk the remaining distance on foot.

3. If your work involves walking around the workplace, it is a healthy sign. However, if your job involves sitting in a cubicle for long hours, try taking breaks frequently and walk around.

4. The lunch break is an excellent opportunity to involve in a brisk walk that helps in generating needed energy to which results in increased attentiveness, focus, and a happy mood for the remainder of your working day.

5. Visit the grocery stores on foot.

6. Walk the children to the school. Walk the dog.

number of steps in a day. Learn to keep track of the number of steps in a day. Note down the steps, and the distance covered. Regular record keeps your momentum up and entitles you to reach your goal with determination. Fitbit Inc is a leading company offering a variety of activity trackers. **Get yourself a tracking system and monitor all the physical activity that you carry out in a day.** A gradual increase in physical activity keeps you strong, motivated, determined, and healthy. Since your mood remains at ease, you are more likely to handle difficult situations with ease.

On average a person walks 100 steps every minute they walk. 10,000 steps per day is equivalent to 100 minutes or 1 hour and 40 minutes of walking. All elite athletes are asked to complete 18,000 steps per day. This maintains their lower limb conditioning and agility.

Another critical outcome of walking is its ability to **enhance your mood to the positive side.** Additionally, you will gain the capacity to focus and stay alert, which is a much needed element to overcome any difficulty that you face in your daily life and the future.

In order to keep the motivation to walk, you can even seek the help of the **technological gadgets** that are available today. The pedometer is the best example. You can strap it to the belt or wear it as a wristband and record the total

Running

Running increases the heart rate drastically and tones the muscles perfectly. In addition, running improves organ-function. The pace at which you run defines the amount of calories burnt. However, it is crucial to consider your body weight, height, medical conditions, and others factors before planning a program. Speaking with your doctor or medical professional will assist you if you are unsure.

Physiotherapists, once again, offer the assistance needed in preparing the running workout program. They also help in aligning your posture. Attaining the right posture has an immense impact on the muscular structure. Malaligned posture causes stress on the muscles, as they have to hold the body in an upright position. In doing this, they seek increased energy, which eventually drains portion of it from the body.

LEARN TO KEEP TRACK OF THE NUMBER OF STEPS IN A DAY.

You will feel exhausted within a short period. Learning to balance the body is critical. It also improves your state of mind.

Spend time walking and running in the presence of the nature. It greatly enhances your mental state, which has a direct impact on your physical state. Furthermore, the freshness of the air and the green surroundings elevates your spirits.

Treadmills give you the chance to carry out the exercise right at your home. It is suitable if you have less time to spend on outdoor exercises. You can choose from a variety of models available in the market. They come with the two set-up options – regular and inclination. You can use the inclination position after you are comfortable running the normal set-up. Inclination elevates your endurance and assists in building muscle mass. The enhanced muscle mass offers the needful activity of burning further calories than the usual. The entire process keeps you healthy and energetic at all times.

Exercise bike

Cycling is another exercise that greatly improves health. Cycling builds endurance and strengthens the core and thigh muscles. If you are suffering from obesity, cycling is one of the best activities to reduce it within a short period. In the beginning, the form of exercise utilizes all the stored fat content from the body.

Shadow boxing

Shadow boxing is a combat sport built for elevating endurance and fitness. This exercise helps in preparing the muscles that increases control in the power you produce. You are the sole participant and you throw punches in a coordinated fashion whilst standing in a slightly side on posture. Most trainers support the activity as an essential element before beginning any other routine exercises. It improves the overall balance of the body and ensures complete control over all the senses. The method involves rocking the body and shuffling back and forth. In terms of psychology, shadow boxing allows a person to overcome their negative self-image.

Swimming

Swimming is another physical activity that supports the development of good health. As an activity, it concentrates on improving endurance, resistance, muscle strength, and an enriched mental state. The low-impact workout proves to be advantageous and one of the best methods to calm down and feel good. Furthermore, it helps in building a healthy circulation system. The recreational activity consists of different styles and uses different motions. All the techniques concentrate on moving ahead with the pace. Butterfly, Backstroke, Breaststroke, and Freestyle are the styles of choice. Each action improves the physical activity with effect on different parts of the body.

Rowing

The rowing action increases cardiovascular strength and is a strong fitness regimen. It is a total body workout because it requires equal effort even from the lower part of the body. Therefore, the entire body, both the upper and lower body exerts equal effort and stress, leading to a greater gain in cardiovascular fitness.

It is crucial to perform the exercise with experts' advice. The posture is entirely different, and any malalignment leads to muscular stress and back pain.

Begin the activity with a reduced pace. Increase the pace and build the resistance. They also support in enhancing the flexibility of the lower and upper body, which increase the efficiency to burn fat at a faster rate.

✤ ✤ ✤

Take charge of your health today and enjoy a happy life. Indulging in physical activity keeps the momentum and the positive attitude that you require to overcome a challenge in your life. Exercises give you the chance to build strength, endurance, focus, and self-confidence. Begin with shorter goals and take a moment to enjoy their achievement. Such an act helps you in boosting your self-confidence, which has an immense effect on your thinking and approach towards life.

Elite athletes follow a schedule that helps them achieve the goals they have set. The program consists of a plan beginning with a simple form of exercise. They slowly move towards complex activities, which increase endurance and fitness. You can begin the week with physical exercises that are relatively easy and then by the end of the week make the program more difficult – testing your skill set further.

Physical activity alone does not help in achieving the health benefits. It is also crucial to follow a diet chart that synchronizes with the exercise regimen. Make sure to consult a dietician. In order to develop a diet chart that suits to your metabolism. Most of the diet charts concentrate on breaking down the eating habit into six times a day. You will eat less quantity in increased intervals. Such a step helps the body to receive the required fuel to produce energy consistently. Inclusion of fibre and protein rich foods improves digestion system that further assists in smooth functioning of the digestion.

The energy that you receive consistently throughout the day keeps you in good health and good state of mind. You will feel refreshed and fit, which keeps you going through all the challenges that you might face in a day. Additionally, you will claim the potential to handle any situation with ease, and remain calm. The reduced stress on the body avoids the occurrence of diseases, which in turn keeps you energetic throughout the day. The availability of the energy at the right intervals of time gives you the opportunity to expand at work and spend quality of time with your loved ones.

Jeremy, a 22 year old national cyclist, loves his sport and is away in Europe and North America for most of the year training and competing. During the final year of his Masters he had to commit to staying in Australia to complete his studies. So what could he do during the off season? The fittest of athletes are the cross country skiers, rowers, swimmers, cyclists, boxers and runners. All he had to do was choose one of these and continue to cross train. He was an excellent swimmer when he was in his early teens and he enjoyed sparring with his friends. Three to six times a week he would swim and do boxing. This helped him continue to be fit, improved his mental preparation and once he graduated he went back into his full cycling training seamlessly.

B. Building your core

Physical exercises improve the flexibility and reduce stress in the body. Nevertheless, there is also a necessity to concentrate on core muscles in order to strengthen them and provide the required strength necessary for the muscular and skeletal structure. Core muscles are responsible for increasing the metabolism rate and offer the required support in holding the body in an upright position.

Core exercises include a variety of physical activities that especially concentrate on abdominal and back muscles. It is essential to improving the strength in this region, as it enables you to carry out everyday tasks with ease. Additionally, strengthening the muscular section in this region prevents the occurrence of back pain. You will also learn the ability to balance your body and maintain the right posture. The simple routine is a 15-minute workout, four times a week, which strengthens the core and tones the midsection of the body.

YOU CAN BEGIN THE WEEK WITH PHYSICAL EXERCISES THAT ARE RELATIVELY EASY.

1. Pilates

Joseph Pilates developed Pilates as a physical fitness in the early 20th century. According to statistics, around 11 million people practice Pilates in the United States alone. There are over 14,000 instructors in the United States. Joseph termed this physical fitness as a method of "Contrology".

According to Joseph Pilates, the physical activity is a combination of mental and physical health. The two important aspects aim at improving the strength of the body, mind, and soul. He steadied eastern and western forms of exercises along with yoga.

Joseph accompanied his method along with the use of a variety of equipment. The apparatus were helpful in accelerating the strengthening, stretching, and body alignment. The use of the equipment and the form of exercise has gained momentum across nations, as it greatly helps in the recovery of injury.

The health benefits associated with the practice of Pilates is an improvement in posture, flexibility, muscle toning, core strengthening, and joint mobility. Additionally, the exercises aim at reducing tension and stress at several joints and junctions, giving freshness to the muscular and skeletal structure.

There is evidence that Pilates is helpful in reducing back pain. However, in order to receive the effectiveness of the physical activity, it is important for you to approach a qualified instructor and receive a tailor-made guidance. They consider the body mass, your medical condition, flexibility, and other criterions that help the instructor to design exercises suitable for your physical ability.

Although Pilates aims at improving the core muscular structure and flexibility, it also acts as a streamlined appearance for weight loss. It is important to combine Pilates along with other weight loss activities such as walking, cycling, and swimming to receive the maximum benefit. It is also vital to contemplate your diet.

Due to its versatility, the age and sex of the person does not restrict who can use Pilates. In some instances Pilates can be practiced well into your 90s. All you need is a tailored exercise program that concentrates on improving your posture, strengthening muscles, and stability. Older clients receive added concentration on body balance and posture.

It is beneficial for people with a lesser active lifestyle and reduced mobility. Participating in Pilates increases activeness and can raise the fitness levels. However, make sure to speak with a health professional before beginning the activity if you have health concerns.

Joseph Pilates initially developed the exercises with the use of his apparatus. He eventually specialized in developing mat exercises to allow every individual to perform and practice Pilates at home. Classes are available from recognized instructors to offer group sessions. The limited number of attendees makes it easy for the instructors to provide a higher level of individual attention. You have the choice of joining a class or hiring an instructor to learn Pilates.

2. Yoga

Yoga is a spiritual, physical, and mental practice that involves a variety of practices and goals. The origin of yoga date backs to the pre-Vedic Indian traditions. It is necessary to impart health to both the mental and physical proportions of the human body. The enthusiasm in the life portrays how healthy you are.

According to Yoga, ill health and sickness are impurities at the state of the mind. They also create distress and discomfort. Therefore, it is vital to treat them as an illness. Body, mind, and soul act as a tripod. If any one aspect is not functioning to its maximum potential, life is out of balance and will lead to the development of ill health. Yoga gives you the opportunity to create harmony by aligning the three components into a single entity.

The Yoga Asanas are physical movements of the body with precise accuracy. Every action calms down the system and improves the breathing. Additionally, the physical movements improve flexibility of the muscular structure, which in turn remove the stress and pressure from within the body. Yoga can fight against lifestyle diseases such as obesity, allergies, hypertension, and stress.

DUE TO ITS VERSATILITY, THE AGE AND SEX OF THE PERSON DOES NOT RESTRICT WHO CAN USE PILATES.

Yoga consists of around 84 poses that concentrate on improving the three components of a person. If you are a beginner it is necessary for you to practice all the postures in a systematic way. The beginning of the exercise concentrates on with simpler tasks that give you the possibility to flex your body. Every human body is different, and yoga gives you the power to identify the best actions that you can carry to improve it.

The yoga positions are available in different groups for beginners. It is preferable to consult a qualified yoga teacher who would instruct the sequence of yoga stretches, standing poses, supine poses, sitting poses, prone poses and meditation.

The different poses concentrate on different aspects of body and mind. Carrying out the exercises improves flexibility and attains balance in life. Further, you will learn the ability to control all the senses, which gives you the inner strength necessary to fight against the odds in life. The increasing work pressure and fast-paced life has reduced the quality of life. With the help of yoga, regaining the lost quality of life is possible. The flexibility achieved through the yoga poses improves blood circulation and oxygen intake.

The improved blood circulation and oxygen intake increases the functionality of the organs and cells in the body. Due to this, the brain activity increases drastically, giving a fresh lease of life. According to studies, the yoga asanas improve concentration levels, grasping power, memory skills, and focus. Including this with physical exercises on daily basis will improve your health and give you the possibility to stay energetic and enthusiastic throughout the day.

Ashtanga and power yoga involves a lot of physical activities. These styles strike a pose for improvement in strength. With an increase in the strength and muscular flexibility, you attain better posture that reduces stress on the entire muscular structure. With a stronger core development, you are likely to sit and stand tall that support and maintain each pose. Yoga also gives you the opportunity to learn about your body. You will be in a position to notice quickly about slumping or slouching so that you can add just the posture to the preferred alignment.

The meditation technique offered by yoga exercises help you immediately in calming the mind. All you ought to do is spend a mere five or ten minutes that will help you gain control over your thoughts. You can apply it at any point during the day or even at the workplace when you feel burdened.

The yoga poses have an immense effect on blood pressure and lowering the heart rate. The lower heart rate is beneficial for people suffering from high blood pressure and other heart diseases. The exercise also helps in improving high-density lipoprotein, which is the good cholesterol. The calming state of mind and the healthy blood circulatory system improves the immune system that acts against several diseases.

Include Yoga exercises in your daily life to enhance your state of mind and achieve control over the senses. You will attain the ability to lead the life in a healthy way and build the necessary inner strength to move against every challenge that you may face in daily life.

3. Tai Chi

Tai Chi combines gentle body movements with deep breathing to achieve relaxation. Originally built as a martial art in the 13th century, Tai Chi today serves as a health promoting exercise around the globe.

The health gains associated with Tai Chi are numerous. According to studies, Tai Chi has an immense effect on people above 65 years old. It assists in reducing the stress, improving the balance and mobility. It also helps in sustaining the muscle strength in the legs, which is crucial for the elderly people.

Speaking about the effects of Tai Chi in the younger generation, the combination of breathing exercises and slow movements, induce the state of calmness and the ability to concentrate on the body. The slow movement activity gives you the power to increase your focus on a particular portion of the body and gain control over it. In addition, the control of the breathing during the activity improves blood circulation and oxygen intake. Altogether, the exercise relaxes all the three components of the human system - body, mind, and soul.

THE BELIEF SYSTEM OF THE TAI CHI INDICATES ITS TWO PRINCIPAL COMPONENTS:

a. Qi - it is an energy force, which flows through the body. The practice of Tai Chi believes in unlocking it in a proper way and redirects it in the right direction.

b. Yin and Yang - Tai Chi believes that the universe consists of opposing elements called as Yin and Yang. It promotes harmony between the two opposing elements to create a balance, which is necessary for any living system in the universe.

Tai Chi classes include warm up session, instruction and practice of Tai Chi forms, and Qigong. The warm up session consists of circular motions such as turning the head from side to side, shoulder circles, rocking back and forth the ankles and so on. The warm up session focuses on loosening the muscles and improves the breathing.

The practice of Tai Chi forms consists of movements with the control over the breathing. Different styles incorporate various movements. They can be smaller or larger movements. As a beginner, you will learn short forms that include slower movements.

Qigong concentrates on improving the energy development and works on the breathing system. The series of actions and motions consists of a few minutes of gentle breathing combined with the slow movement. The primary aim of Qigong is to help relax the mind and muster the energy of the body. The practice includes lying down, sitting, or standing.

As Tai Chi is a slow and gentle form of physical activity, it does not leave you breathless. Instead, it concentrates on the components of body balance, muscle strength, and flexibility. According to a study conducted by Stanford University, participating in thirty-six Tai Chi classes over a period of twelve weeks resulted in reducing cardiovascular diseases. Additionally, patients displayed improvement in both upper and lower body strength. There was a significant impact on burning unwanted calories in the body. In another study carried out in Japan, Tai Chi improved the lower body strength by 30% and arm strength by 25%. An important element of Tai Chi is its ability to strengthen the core muscles of the abdomen and back. It builds the resistance without the use of weights.

A significant impact observed in Tai Chi is its ability to improve the body balance. The control of the senses, breathing system, and the continual activity of motion gives

THE PRACTICE OF TAI CHI FORMS CONSISTS OF MOVEMENTS WITH THE CONTROL OVER THE BREATHING.

the capacity to increase alertness. It in turn improves brain functionality, which is responsible for controlling the entire body. Tai Chi helps in training the sensory neurons and stretch receptors, which act as a feedback in the body balance. In some studies, Tai Chi also assisted in reducing the fear of falling in elderly people.

Depending on the form of style and the size of the moment, Tai Chi can provide a few aerobic benefits. It is relevant for you to consult a doctor before beginning any physical activity, considering that you have a medical condition. They provide you an insight about the intensity required for the cardiovascular activity. If they suggest a workout with reduced heart rate, Tai Chi is the best form of physical activity.

4. Hydrotherapy

Formerly called hydropathy, hydrotherapy is a form of medicine that involves the use of water for treating pains. It encompasses a broad range of therapeutic methods and approaches that utilize the advantage of water properties such as pressure and temperature stimulate blood circulation and offer treatment to a particular set of diseases.

The present day, hydrotherapy utilizes water jets, underwater massage, and mineral baths. Other forms include whirlpool bath, hot Roman bath, cold plunge, Jacuzzi, and hot tub. Although restricted to use in physical therapy, using hydrotherapy as a form of treatment is to deliver heat and cold to the body. It is also the primary application of the procedure. The methods and techniques involved facilitate thermoregulatory reactions that calm the state of mind and helps in regulating the blood circulation at its maximum potential.

Before beginning the use of hydrotherapy, it is necessary to consult a physician. In most cases, the treatment includes with the assistance from some physiotherapy departments. The physiotherapist will display an array of exercises that focus on improving the strength of the muscles, release stress, and achieve the state of calmness. The exercises and the movements are tailor-made and change according to your symptoms.

The physical exercises involve movements of the body in warm water. The unique properties of the water improve the swollen joints, provide relaxation, strengthen weak muscles, and alleviate pains and aches.

Hydrotherapy gives you the opportunity to relieve muscle spasm and pain. The buoyancy of the water relaxes the tight muscles and reduces the weight at various painful joints. It also aids in blood circulation, which acts as a supportive environment for rehabilitation. In addition, due to the reduction in the gravity, the favourable properties of the water make it easy to relieve stress and allow free movement of the body, which is difficult on land.

The water pressure and the warm temperature together constitute to a custom-built session that stimulates the circulatory system and encourages the disposal of waste products from the body. The ability to exercise and move freely in the water boosts motivation and promotes well-being. The warm water acts as the source for relaxation and soothing effect. Furthermore, the warm temperature of the pool improves general fitness and health, aiding improvement in the cardiovascular fitness.

Majority of spa holidays offer various hydrotherapy suites that give you the opportunity to take the advantage of the numerous positive effects of the water therapy. The alternating variation of water temperature works like a charm in reducing inflammation, stimulating, soothing, and calming all the senses.

An important element that you will receive by undergoing the hydrotherapy is the boost to the immune system. Increasing the immune system is an essential aspect of any person. The immune system is the barrier against the disease-causing bacteria within the body. At the same time, the body regains its ability to detoxify naturally. You will experience an increase in sweating, which is the way out for the impurities from within the body.

Several hospitals and recreational centers are now offering hydrotherapy. You will receive the many benefits of water therapy, which will assist you in improving the functioning of all the senses of the human body. It will in turn give you the possibility to approach any activity in a positive manner.

C. Eating the "right" food

Eating good food in the required quantities has its own benefits on the human system. Apart from providing the needed energy at regular intervals, eating good food also assists in weight loss. The human system requires a good portion of supplements to keep the internal and external system on the right track. Healthy eating does not constitute to the strict dietary limitations and staying thin. Depriving the body of the useful foods complicates further the health issues.

Eating good food concentrates on consuming the food that will make you feel great and give you an ample amount of energy. Many people are overwhelmed and find the amount of diet and nutritional advice out there confusing. You will come across a myriad of statements that are conflicting and confusing. The following will provide you with the useful information with which you can quickly learn to eat healthy food that is tasty, varied, and a health-conscious diet.

KEY EATING TIPS FOR YOU FROM KUSAL GOONEWARDENA

Tip 1:

In order to be prosperous, it is essential to plan a healthy diet as manageable steps rather than a drastic change.

✢ Simplified: Rather than counting the total number of calories consumed in a single day, you can select other measuring options like colour, variety, and freshness. The changes give you easier healthy choices. You can concentrate on foods that you love and the recipes that incorporate fresh ingredients.

✢ Start slowly: Changing the diet plan immediately overnight is not realistic. In fact, an immediate change in your eating pattern displays your unwillingness to incorporate the new eating plan. Begin with small steps to the diet and switchover from butter to olive oil while cooking. These little instances become a regular habit, and you can continue to add more healthy choices as you proceed.

✢ Focus on post-eating feelings: focusing on this is an essential tool to develop new habits and tastes. Furthermore, it will give you an insight into the products that make you feel good at any point in time. However, you have to observe that the more consumption of junk food is likely to cause you discomfort, nausea, and being drained of energy. Try to stay away from junk food and include natural foods that keep you energetic throughout the day.

✤ Elimination: you do not have to eliminate every food that you do not enjoy. The important aspect of consuming all the vegetables and fruits is to receive a feel-good factor, reduce risk of heart attack and cancer causing elements, and produce energy at frequent intervals. Make sure that the food choices that you make are healthy and offer you the happy state of mind that you wish to possess at all times.

Tip 2:

Moderation is an important element that enables any healthy diet to offer the best advantages. Moderation defines the limitation of consuming food according to the requirement of the body needs. It is imperative that you feel satisfied at the end of the meal rather than acquiring a feeling of burden. Moderation also speaks about balance. The human system requires a balanced diet that consists of carbohydrates, protein, fat, fibre, vitamins, and minerals. All these components sustain a healthy body and ensure proper functioning of the system.

The goal of eating healthy depends upon the diet chart prepared according to your lifestyle. Furthermore, the diet chart is for the rest of the life but not for a few weeks or months. The diet chart concentrates on replacing the unhealthy stuff with healthy products. It does not mean that you have to eliminate the foods that you love eating. For example, you can have bacon for breakfast twice a week, which is moderation. Simply follow a healthy lunch and dinner to keep the health in its right form.

Do not limit any food products. When you ban or keep certain foods out of reach, it is the human tendency to want those foods the most. Rather than banning the food products, minimize the portions of consumption. For example, you can consume a burger and a packet of chips once a week, as it does not have a larger impact on the health. It holds true when you are in a position to carry out the diet chart as scheduled for the rest of the days. With reduced intake of unhealthy foods, you will find yourself craving for them with less enthusiasm and treat them as occasional indulgences.

It is always beneficial to think about smaller portions. When dining out, make sure to begin with a starter and shared with a friend or colleague. Do not look at super-sized quantities. Even at home, use smaller plates, which have a realistic serving size. If you are unsatisfied with the meal, you can round off by adding fresh fruits. Try to relate the portions of the servings to objects. For example, the portion sizes of meat, fish, and chicken will be the size of deck cards. Pasta, rice, or mashed potato is about the size of a traditional light bulb. Such variation and imagination give you a firm command over your senses and the eating habits.

IT IS IMPERATIVE THAT YOU FEEL SATISFIED AT THE END OF THE MEAL RATHER THAN ACQUIRING A FEELING OF BURDEN.

Tip 3:

Apart from eating the right food ingredients, emphasis is also, on how you eat it. It includes your thoughts and the feel-good factor about the food that you are about to consume. You will have to foster the habit of thinking about food as nourishment rather than something to gulp down at the lunch hour.

Try to eat with your colleagues, friends, or family members. Eating with people has numerous emotional benefits. It especially holds true for children, as it gives the ability to build a model of healthy eating habits. Consuming food in front of a television or computer leads to endless overeating, which significantly affects the digestive system and your thoughts.

Another important aspect is to enjoy your meal times. Savour every bite and chew the food slowly. The mad rush of office hours devoid the opportunity to taste the flavours and feel the textures of the food. Try to eat slowly and reconnect with the joy of eating.

It is not important to consume food according to the lunch breaks and dinnertime. You have to attend to your body and ask if it is hungry. You can check this by drinking a glass of water. It needs a few minutes for the brain to tell the body that it is full. Make sure to reduce the intake at the end of the meal and cause for a moment to check whether the body is full or not.

Breakfast is an important meal of the day. A healthy breakfast in the appropriate quantity starts the metabolism on the more youthful front. Additionally, eating small healthy meals throughout the day maintains the required energy development and metabolism.

It is also preferable to avoid eating at night. Try to consume your dinner before 6 PM when your metabolism is at its peak stage. Leaving a gap of 12 to 14 hours until the next morning breakfast usually helps the digestive system to function smoothly. If you feel hungry, consume liquids such as soups, fruit juices, and water. They have less fat content and do not add to the calories.

Tip 4:

Include colourful foods rather than counting the calories. **Fruits and vegetables are a rich source of essential nutrients.** They also form the foundation for a healthy diet. Many people fall short of the recommended daily consumption of five variants of fruits and vegetables. Try to increase the brightness by adding more of fruits and vegetables - the brighter, the better. Fruits and vegetables have high concentrations of minerals, vitamins, and antioxidants. Add berries to your breakfast or eat a fruit as a healthy dessert. Snack carrots or cherry tomatoes rather than processed snack foods.

Chinese cabbage, broccoli, green lettuce, and mustard greens are high in calcium, potassium, iron, magnesium, and vitamins A, C, E, and K. Natural sweet vegetables such as carrots, sweet potatoes, onions, corn, and squash act as natural sweeteners to your meal. They will assist in the reduction of the craving for sweets or desserts after a meal. Fruits are rich reservoirs of antioxidants, vitamins, and fibre. They are a perfect way to fill up and satisfy a meal. Berries contain **cancer-fighting elements** while apples provide fibre, which improves the digestion system. Every fruit is a rich source of a particular vitamin. Consuming fruits after a meal or during a break is a wonderful way to enrich your mood and health.

Maintaining a daily regimen of nutritional supplements has a significant impact on your eating habits. It is because the benefits of fruits and vegetables do not come from a single or isolated antioxidant. The benefits obtained from vegetables and fruits come from several vitamins, minerals, and phytochemicals that work together simultaneously.

Tip 5:

The human body demands its share of carbohydrates. Consuming fibre is also essential to maintain a healthy digestive system. Whole grains are rich sources of healthy carbohydrates and fibre. They also provide the long-lasting energy required for you to remain active throughout the day. In addition to their satisfying nature, whole grains are also rich sources of antioxidants and phytochemicals. These two components protect you against cancer causing elements, diabetes, and coronary heart diseases.

Healthy carbohydrates, also called good carbs, are available abundantly in whole grains, beans, fruits, and vegetables. Good sources of carbohydrates digest slowly. Due to this, you will **feel full for an extended period,** which keeps the insulin and blood sugar levels in the stable level.

Unhealthy carbohydrates, or bad carbs, are abundantly available in refined sugar, white flour, and white rice. Stripping of bran, nutrients, and fibre is the process that results in white rice. Unhealthy carbohydrates increase blood sugar levels and digest quickly. Due to this, you will consume food more than the body requires.

✣ Make sure you add a variety of whole grains in the healthy diet. Include Brown rice and whole wheat.

✣ Make sure you are getting the right whole grains from the market. Words can be misleading and there is a lot of difference between whole grain and 100% whole grain.

✣ Being accustomed to the new food ingredient can be troublesome in the beginning. Begin by mixing a variety of whole grains that you use. You can gradually increase the use of 100% whole grains.

Tip 6:

Like carbohydrates, fats can also be categorized as good and bad. **Consumption of the healthy fats is necessary for the human body to nourish the brain, heart, and cells.** In addition, they also provide the necessary moisturization required for the skin, hair, and nails. Foods that are rich in omega-3 are important and have the ability to reduce cardiovascular diseases. Furthermore, omega-3 has the power to alter your mood. Additionally, omega-3 is a useful ingredient in avoiding the occurrence of dementia.

Monosaturated fats: plant oils like canola oil, peanut oil, and olive oil are rich sources of monosaturated fats. Avocados and nuts, such as hazelnuts, pecans, and almonds are also the rich sources of the monosaturated fats.

Polyunsaturated fats with **omega-3 and omega-6 fatty acids:** omega-3 and omega-6 are rich in fatty fish such as salmon, herring, sardines, anchovies, and a few cold-water fish oil supplements. Other sources include unheated sunflower, soybean, corn, walnuts, and flaxseed oils.

FRUITS AND VEGETABLES HAVE HIGH CONCENTRATIONS OF MINERALS, VITAMINS, AND ANTIOXIDANTS.

It is vital for you to reduce or **eliminate saturated fats and trans fats** from your diet chart. Whole milk products and red meat are rich sources of saturated fats. Crackers, candies, snack foods, baked goods, fried food products, and other processed foods are rich sources of trans fats. Eliminating them is vital to ensure good health.

Tip 7:

Adding calcium to your daily diet enhances the skeletal structure. **Calcium is an essential ingredient in improving the bone health.** It is necessary for the structure to have the appropriate quantity of calcium to remain healthy and provide you with enough support. The body uses the availability of calcium to build healthy bones and teeth and sends messages through the nervous system, as you age. It also helps in regulating the heart's rhythm. If there is less intake of calcium, the body utilizes the available calcium from the bones to ensure normal functioning of the cells. Such a situation leads to osteoporosis and arthritis.

The recommended levels of calcium are 1000mg per day. It goes above 1200mg if you are above fifty years of age. Make sure to include foods that provide you the required calcium. Under critical circumstances, you can choose low-dose calcium supplements in order to make up for the shortfall. Apart from increasing the intake of calcium-rich foods, it is also necessary to **avoid foods that deplete the body's calcium.** Alcohol, caffeine, and aerated drinks consume calcium from the bones. Weight bearing exercises and consumption of the required doses of magnesium and vitamins D and K help in regulating the activity of calcium.

Dairy products are rich sources of calcium. The body digests the dairy products comfortably and absorbs the calcium with ease. Dairy products include milk, cheese, and yogurt. Green leafy vegetables are abundant reservoirs of calcium. Broccoli, cabbage, summer squash, mustard greens, turnip greens, kale, celery, green beans, asparagus, and Brussels sprouts are the best sources of calcium. White beans, black-eyed peas, kidney beans, and pinto beans are also rich sources of calcium. Include these products in your daily diet chart to ensure that the body receives the required share of calcium.

ALCOHOL, CAFFEINE, AND AERATED DRINKS CONSUME CALCIUM FROM THE BONES.

Tip 8:

Protein is an essential aspect of the human body. It gives you the energy to perform several activities in the day. The digestive system breaks down the protein available in the food into twenty amino acids. These amino acids are the building blocks for growth and energy development. Amino acids serve a central role in supporting healthy tissues, cells, and organs. However, keeping a watch over the intake of protein is crucial. Excessive intake leads to kidney diseases. According to latest studies, we require high-quality protein compared to the current dietary recommendations. In another study, the results displayed an increase in the intake of protein with increase in age. The increased protein maintains the physical activity to the normal condition, when the body ages.

The requirement of the protein is weight-based rather than calorie intake. Studies reveal that adults require at least 0.8 g of lean and high-quality protein per kilogram. Therefore, you will have to measure the requirement according to your body weight. A small increase in the quantity assists in lowering the risk of developing osteoporosis, obesity, heart stroke, and type II diabetes. It is also crucial to divide the intake equally among all the meals. Nursing women require about 20 g high-quality protein than their daily requirement during pregnancy, in order to support milk production.

The critical aspect of consuming high-quality protein is by altering the food ingredients. Do not rely solely on milk, dairy products, and red meat. Replacing the processed carbohydrates with high-quality protein improves the good cholesterol, which in turn reduces the risk of heart diseases. In addition, consumption of high-quality protein keeps you full at all times and aids in weight loss.

You can begin by replacing red meat with fish and chicken. Include plant- based protein such as nuts, beans, and soy. Avoid processed carbohydrates that are abundant in cakes, pizza, cookies, pastries, and chips. Replace these products with beans, fish, chicken, low-fat dairy products, and soy products. You can additionally choose grilled chicken breast with beans rather than slices of pizza.

Tip 9:

Learning to limit the intake of salt and sugar is advantages. If you are successful in planning your diet with increased fibre rich fruits and vegetables along with whole grains, good fats, and protein, you will find yourself moving towards good health by **cutting down excessive intake of salt and sugar.**

An increased intake of sugar causes spikes in energy development. Additionally, it adds to the weight and health problems. Even if you eliminate cakes, candies, and desserts, you will still have a long way ahead to cut down the sugar level. It is because a large amount of sugar is available in a hidden format. Breads, canned soups, canned vegetables, pasta sauce, instant mashed potatoes, fast food, ketchup, and soy sauce have hidden sugar levels.

A better way to reduce the risk of sugar intake is by **eliminating sugary drinks.** For example, one bottle of soda has ten teaspoons of sugar. It exceeds the daily-recommended level. Therefore, you can switch to sparkling water with lemon or fruit juice. Unsweetened foods such as iced tea, unflavoured oatmeal, and plain yogurt have no sugar levels. You can sweeten the products by adding fruits, which are the natural sweeteners. Natural peanut butter, fruits, and peppers are naturally sweet foods that will satisfy your sweet requirement. Make sure to keep these products handy rather than depending on cookies and candies.

You are bound to consume excessive intake of salt rather than the recommended level. An increase in the salt intake results in high blood pressure that leads to different health problems. **You will have to limit the sodium intake to 1,500 mg per day.** A better way to begin is by avoiding processed and pre-packaged to foods. Frozen dinners and canned soups are rich sources of salts that exceed the recommended levels. Fast foods are rich in sodium salts. A few restaurants also utilize excessive salt to retain the flavour of the recipe. If possible, you can seek the recipe without salt. You can also ask for gravy and sauces without salt. Instead, you can seek table salt, where you can add a little, or a pinch to taste. This way, you will significantly reduce the intake of sodium salt.

Choose fresh fruits and vegetables rather than canned vegetables. Reduce your grocery requirements on potato chips, pretzels, and nuts. Check the label and search for the salt content, before buying a product. Choose a low salt or reduced sodium product that will limit your salt intake. Additionally, you can even decrease the use of salt at home. Begin slowly and let the taste buds at just to the new schedule.

Tip 10:

It is essential to include foods that are rich in dietary fibre. Dietary fibre assists in lowering heart diseases, heart strokes, and diabetes. Additionally, it supports weight loss. The recommended levels change between 21 and 38 g of fibre per day, depending on your age and medical conditions.

You will increase the intake if you choose more of natural food than unprocessed food. Natural foods are rich in fibre. Good sources of fibre include wheat cereals, whole grains, oatmeal, and barley, vegetables such as celery, tomatoes, carrots, and fruits such as apples, berries, and pears.

A better way to add fibre to your daily diet is by beginning the day with a wholegrain cereal. You can also add unprocessed wheat bran or by adding all bran cereal. With an increased intake of fibre content, you will remain at full status for a longer period. In this way, you will consume less food that also helps in controlling the weight. In addition, fibre also helps in moving excessive fat content through the digestive system at a faster rate. When you fill up on high-fibre foods, you will receive the needed energy to participate actively in any exercise.

EVEN IF YOU ELIMINATE CAKES, CANDIES, AND DESSERTS, YOU WILL STILL HAVE A LONG WAY AHEAD TO CUT DOWN THE SUGAR LEVEL.

CHAPTER 3

ACHIEVING POTENTIAL –
LIMITATIONS, BARRIERS, AND SOLUTIONS

Every individual has a rotating life, comprised of waking up, going to the workplace, returning home and going to bed. This routine is an everyday activity for millions of people across the globe. People tend to follow it as a schedule because the actions become a comfort zone. It is less challenging, and they find it comforting as it fulfils their daily requirements. Irrespective of your innate talents or family background, reaching the stage you want is purely dependent on your potential.

We all have our potential. It is a mad mixture of environment, genetics, and the body's design that each one is different from another. Sometimes, environment also has a role in deviating from the goal of success. For example, you might have lived in an area with fewer options or had no money for a class. It would've been difficult for you to experience the things that you are naturally good at

In a few instances, ambition, mixed with a false belief can also get in the way of success. Adding further to those woes is circumstances. If you are struggling with finances and have a family to support, you will find it difficult to make your way out of it and find the key to the missing success.

"IT'S THE SUCCESS STORY OF EVERY SUCCESSFUL MAN'S LIFE. YOU HAVE TO BREAK THAT ROUTINE FACTOR TO ACHIEVE SUCCESS AND TASTE NEW DIMENSIONS OF THE LIFE. PEOPLE WHO BECOME SUCCESSFUL MOVE AHEAD WITH PASSION AND POSSESS THE ABILITY TO LEARN NEW THINGS. IT GIVES THEM THE OPPORTUNITY TO DEVELOP NEW TALENTS, WHICH THEY LIVE AND BREATHE IN ORDER TO FULFIL THEIR DREAMS."

– KUSAL

SELF-DEPRECATION AND LACK-FOCUS

So what is self-deprecation?

Let's think for a few moments about self-love. When we are being loving towards ourselves, we are supporting the goodness within, thinking about what we are grateful for and looking towards a positive future. We are acting as a friend to ourselves.

Self-deprecation is essentially the opposite of self-love. It is the act of demeaning or being hard on yourself, perhaps with some perceived justification but often without any particular reason.

Self-deprecation is generally a masochistic tendency, where we inflict pain and suffering on ourselves with our internal dialogue as well as perhaps with our actions.

Why do we do this? There are many reasons, most of which come from a mindset that focuses on what is lacking. We are not good enough, we do not have enough money, we are not smart enough, we are not handsome and/or pretty enough, we are not successful enough, and if we are not enough then we probably deserve to be treated poorly. Again, it is the opposite of self love. It is finding ways to be harmful to ourselves on the mental, emotional, physical and often spiritual levels.

Brene Brown, researcher, author and speaker, has done tremendous work on the topics of Vulnerability, Shame and Guilt. In her work, she describes this "lack-focus", and how we often start our day thinking about what we are lacking. Lynne Twist, author of *The Soul of Money*, also refers to this focus on 'not enough', or 'insufficiency' thinking. Both describe the feelings of shame and guilt as well as the negative self-perception that can arise from this lack-focus and the problems this can cause not only within us but with others. If there is 'not enough' at the start of the day, then it follows into 'I must not be enough.' And if 'I am not enough' then it follows from that there are simply not enough resources in the world to make me happy, since the problem is within. If there are not enough resources in the world, I'd better get as many as I can before all those

A Personal Experience from Helene Finizio

"When I was in high school I was a part of a clique of friends who were very close and very selective. We all felt very mindful of how we dressed, how we acted, and so on. Growing up in this kind of environment, it is no surprise to hear that eating disorders were quite the norm. Being extra thin for the girls was not only expected, but basically required. We used to have contests to see who could eat the least in a week. The least in a week! I kid you not. That sense of competition and elitism drove us all to some very unhealthy places, so far so that I recall my doctor telling my parents that I 'had to start eating something', and my reply was, 'oh fine!' Self-deprecation takes on many forms, eating disorders are just one of many examples."

other greedy people/groups/countries take what I need.. And on and on it goes.

Seeing the cycle here? When we come from a place of lack, and we are willing to be harsh towards ourselves, we are causing pain not only within, but to others who are interacting with this energy as well. We are much more likely to reinforce this kind of thinking and behaviour in others when we allow it for ourselves, and the cycle continues. This is one of our greatest barriers to mental, emotional, physical, sexual and spiritual well being.

> "IT IS OUR DUTY TO OURSELVES AND TO THE INTERCONNECTED COMMUNITY OF THE WORLD TO LET GO OF THE SELF-DEPRECATING ABUSE CYCLES, TO STEP BEYOND A LACK-MENTALITY, AND TO BECOME BETTER FRIENDS TO OURSELVES AND OUR GLOBAL COMRADES. IT IS OUR DUTY TO BECOME OUR OWN BEST FRIENDS."
>
> – HELENE

I. TOWARDS OPTIMISM AND STRENGTHS

We have a choice about how we think. It may not seem like it at first, but once we begin to tap into a more aware and present relationship with our minds, the thoughts that go through our heads all day, every day, can become our friends at a whim. Once we practice positive thinking enough, our thoughts will naturally shift to a more positive default without us having to do anything. Practice makes perfect, and a little effort in the beginning can go an awfully long way.

What we are really talking about here is becoming more optimistic and strengths-focused. Remember that glass of water? Well with enough patience, self care, and effort we can see that water and be grateful for the half-full glass every time. We can let go of the lack-focus and appreciate where we are, who we are, and what we have. Our weaknesses do not define us. It is our actions, our hearts and our spirits who make us who we are.

"WE ARE STRONG,
BEAUTIFUL PEOPLE,
AND WE DESERVE
TO FEEL LOVE
IN EACH AND
EVERY MOMENT."

– HELENE

Does this mean that problems will not arise? That life will not have challenges and bumps along the way? Of course not. But what this does mean is that we have a choice to allow a current of support and connection with feeling good, knowing the goodness within us, and allowing that presence of goodness to be with us consciously all day every day.

Optimism and a strengths focus will guide us into a deeper relationship with all that is right in ourselves and in the world. They are key ingredients to living a life of Gratitude, Hope and Peace.

And isn't that worth the effort?

II. OTHER PEOPLE MATTER AND HAVING THE RIGHT SOCIAL SUPPORT TEAM

So, if we are going to do all this "work", what do we need in order to be successful at it? What are the key ingredients for our hard work and dedication in creating a more positive focus and more positive behaviours paying off?

Christopher Peterson was one of the smartest people I have ever had the honour of knowing. He was one of the key founders of the field of Positive Psychology, and his work will help generations upon generations. Chris was an avid researcher and scholar, and his brilliance resided not only in his ability to see clearly the important points hiding within tremendous amounts of data, but also his ability to articulate those important points in a way that made sense.

Chris had a saying that was so simple, and yet so powerful, I have shared this with as many people as I possibly could, and here I will share it with you. His simple saying, for which time will never erase the importance, is this:

Other People Matter.

Other.

People.

Matter.

Take a moment, take a breath, and drink this one in. So simple, and so important.

We live in a world with Billions of other people. We were not born into a world of isolation. We were born into a world of interconnection, social organization, interdependence and spiritual camaraderie.

If we are working on being our own best selves, those people in our lives must be a supportive part of that equation.

Along the path of my private practice, I had the opportunity to interview Lodgwick Cook, former CEO of Arco Oil, a Fortune 10 company. When I asked him what his one best tip would be for up-and-coming leaders, he said, "Make sure you have the right team."

These figureheads in academia and business are sharing a wisdom that somewhere within ourselves, we all already know.

We did not come to this lifetime to do everything on our own. We came here to have a human experience, as a part of billions of other people also present here, sharing this human experience with us! Our teams, our friends, our social groups, our soul circles, matter.

And if we have the right people around us, the right support in our lives, we can accomplish our destinies.

III. NEURAL PATHWAYS AND SUBCONSCIOUS TICKER TAPE RUN AMUCK!

The way we think becomes reinforced over time. What we think becomes programmed into our brains, stored in our long-term memory, and wired into our neural pathways. The more we think a thought, the stronger the neural pathway becomes, and the easier it is to access that thought in long-term memory. This is why studying for a test is effective. When we go over a fact over and over again, we have a better chance of accessing that information later on when we need it.

We are thinking machines! We are almost always processing something, be it a thought from within our own psyches, or some information gained from our world. As we mentioned, there are as many as 70,000 thoughts that go through any single human brain every day, or even more!

In Positive Psychology, this constant and infinite flow of thoughts in the brain is referred to as the "ticker tape." Similar to the stock market ticker, where the numbers flow all day long and they continue to go up and down in relationship to buyers, sellers and global happenings, the mental ticker tape is always running. Some thoughts we "buy" into, others we "sell" and let go of, and the happenings in our inner and outer world are constant factors in the thoughts that appear on the screens of our conscious and unconscious minds.

If the ticker tape is left without guidance, our negativity bias can cause us to focus on what is lacking, what is problematic, what went wrong in the past, what isn't correct right now, what we might need to worry about in the future... all.... day.... long. If we let this happen for too many days, the neural pathways in our brains will begin to support this constant stream of negative thinking, and our neurophysiology will begin to support an automatic default to the negative.

Sometimes the negative thoughts originate from simple survival cues early on in our lives.

I did some incredible therapeutic work with Dr. Neal Marshall Goldsmith, a psychotherapist in New York City who specializes in altered states of consciousness. Neal and I were looking

interpretations, and that every time we hear someone yell, or become upset, or even just hear a loud noise, it can reinforce the neural pathway that equates 'loud sound' to 'I might die.'

It may sound too simple, or somewhat silly, but I will tell you, having this insight shared with me **helped me tremendously in dealing with the reverberations of anxiety** associated with the fear-inducing visions I had experienced. This information still helps me keep my emotional reactions in perspective if I find myself anxious and cannot explain why. Neal also used to discuss the importance of 'set and setting', and how visual and auditory cues can be powerful indicators of our emotional response. Are we feeling cold? Is it noisy? Are there colours that bring up memories for us? Are we around people we have known for a year or more and trust? Is there music playing? Do we care for it? All these factors and more can be strong determining factors as to how we interpret our moments from one to the next, and it is up to us to gain the awareness we need to navigate our thoughts, our neurophysiology, our past, present and future thinking with **mindfulness and grace**. It is up to us to become more positive, to become more strengths-and-solutions focused, to bring in more love and light, and to share that with others. It is up to us, as the Hopi Elders so eloquently say, to "Be the change we wish to see in the world".

at some particularly "challenging" visions I had experienced while in a dramatically altered state of awareness. The visions were so powerful, similar to those I had experienced when I was a very young child, and it left me feeling raw, vulnerable, and frightened. We looked at what was going on in my psyche and what imprints had been left there within which the frightening visions could find a 'lock that fit them as a key.' Neal explained to me that when our brain is forming, as early as ages 3-5, if our parents so much as yell at us, we can interpret that as a threat to our survival given that we need them for life support until we are a good deal older. He told me that even before any mature and integrated life experiences, we can **ingrain an intense fight or flight pattern** into our subconscious based on these early-stage developmental

OUR STRENGTHS, OUR NATURAL ABILITIES TO BE, DO AND CREATE THE GOODNESS IN OUR LIVES, ARE LIKE SUNLIGHT.

The time is now.

The knowledge is here.

What is one small step you can take Right Now, In This Moment, to let go of what no longer serves you and create a better mental state?

Even if we simply just take one deep breath….bringing in the good, letting go of what no longer serves us….we are doing our part.

What else can you do for you? And in doing for you, for those around you….

IV. LACK OF STRENGTHS AWARENESS- THE 24 GLOBAL CHARACTER STRENGTHS

When we are focusing on the problems, they can consume us. Going down a rabbit hole, such as the negative thinking spiral, can lead us into a small and dark cavern from which the sunlight is hard to see.

Our strengths, our natural abilities to be, do and create the goodness in our lives, are like sunlight. They are always there, even when we are sleeping. We might not always be able to see them, but that does not mean they are gone from us. They are always within us, always available to be called upon. Just like light, they are present in ways science has yet to fully comprehend. Just like light, they give us strength and the ability to see more clearly how best to navigate our world.

Our strengths are a gift. They may seem overwhelming at times. Marianne Williamson once said it is not so much the dark we fear, but the power of our own light. Our strengths are this light within us. They are vehicles for the expression of the beauty of our human condition as an extension of our spiritual presence.

We are just at the very, very beginning of learning about and knowing about the myriad of strengths within the human psyche. Much like the five senses, we are always discovering more. Five is a starting point for the senses. 24 is a starting point for strengths.

Martin E.P. Seligman and the late and great Christopher Peterson, two of the original founders of the field of Positive Psychology (the psychology of what is Right with you) identified 24 global character strengths pervasive across culture. These are a window into the possibilities of the infinite strengths within us all. When we begin to look at our strengths, we begin to bring our awareness and attention to all that is going Right, and all we are already able to be and do.

"THE BEST PLACE TO SUCCEED IS WHERE YOU ARE WITH WHAT YOU HAVE."

– CHARLES SCHWAB

> "THESE STRENGTHS ALL CONTRIBUTE TO PEAK PERFORMANCE MINDSET THINKING (PPMT)."
>
> – HELENE

As a starting point, let's take a look at the initial 24 global character strengths that Drs Seligman and Peterson identified. As you are reading through these, the titles are coming straight from them, the descriptions from me to you. Take a moment after reading each one and simply see what comes up in your mind. All of what we are about to discuss is already within you.

A. **Curiosity and interest in the world:** This strength is all about our ability to take interest in the world around us, approaching life with a sense of wonder and childlike awe. It is a vantage point of the seeking mind that allows a flourishing of curiosity, and as a strength this can lead us to discovery and experience from which the heart and soul of life is known.

B. **Industry, diligence and perseverance:** This strength depicts our ability to show up, breathe and keep going no matter what is in front of us. Life is filled with opportunities to overcome challenges, professionally and personally. We have within us everything that we need to accomplish the goals at hand, and to handle whatever comes our way.

> "THE HUMAN SPIRIT IS STRONGER THAN ANYTHING THAT CAN HAPPEN TO IT."
>
> – GEORGE C. SCOTT

C. Judgement, critical thinking and open-mindedness: This strength depicts our ability to analyze a situation, a fact, a circumstance, and look at life through a variety of lenses. We are constantly accessing insights and information mentally and spiritually. Our judgements, the way we think about what is present in our lives, and our ability to remain open to possibilities, is an extension of the way in which we are showing up in the world. Our thoughts are an expression of who we are.

D. Creativity, ingenuity and originality: This strength speaks to the flow of life-force energy that is present with us in each and every moment. Sometimes we are aware of it, and sometimes we are not. It is always with us. Our ability to create, to turn a vision into art, to turn a thought into action, to share something unique born of ourselves and no one else, is our ability to let our lives flourish with connect to Love, Light and Source.

E. Citizenship, teamwork and loyalty: This strength is essential to a happy and healthy lifestyle. As we noted Christopher Peterson so often said, 'Other People Matter.' Present in any happy and successful life is a team. We are interconnected and our ability to show up for that interconnection is represented in this strength. When we are able to be loyal to our team, to operate with integrity and a set of moral values that contribute to a sense of citizenship, to work as a united force, the impossible becomes achievable and our lives become a canvas for the masterpieces of our souls.

F. Forgiveness and mercy: This strength is a core ingredient in a healthy mindset. Life is full of challenge points. The world is full of positive and negative experiences. There are many people who are incredibly enlightened, and others who are lost and filled with pain. Many of us have encountered those who truly are in desperate need of mercy. It is our ability to forgive, to express mercy as a way of compassion, which allows us to move through the experiences of strife with grace.

G. Hope, optimism and future-mindedness: Hope is one of the strongest forces in the Universe. It connects us to the presence of God, Source, Love, Light, a Higher Power who cares for us, kindred spirits who are here for us, and people who love us. Optimism is hope in action, the ability to look at what is going right, and think towards the positive outcomes we would most love. Future-mindedness allows us to bring hope and optimism with us into the next moment, and the next, and the next. This strength is the alpha and omega of Peak Performance Mindset Thinking (PPMT).

H. **Zest, enthusiasm and energy:** This strength is about the flow of life force through us as well. Our energy is an extension of our spirit, and our connection to something greater than ourselves. When we are in harmony with our own spirit, we often have the freedom to experience zest, or an excitement for life. Enthusiasm is the joyous extension of that freedom, and we live with a childlike excitement. Life is meant to be enjoyed, and this is a core strength of the Happy Life.

I. **Honesty, authenticity and genuineness:** This strength is about being real with yourself, and when you are ready being real with other people as well. We often try to be someone we are not. We try to please others, to show up in a way that we think others need. What we really need to do is be true to who we are. Honesty starts with an honest conversation within ourselves. Authenticity is the ability to show up from that space of honesty. Genuineness is the ability to share that authenticity with others. This strength requires a trust that we are perfect just as we are. That we are enough. And that we will connect with those people we are meant to connect with.

J. **Appreciation of beauty and excellence:** Beauty is an extension of our spirit. Be it beauty of an individual, beauty in an artistic creation, or simply beauty in the moment, the experience of beauty is the experience of beauty made manifest. Excellence is the commitment to show up fully with the truth of our beauty shared honestly and openly. Excellence is a commitment to be he or she who we came here to be. Beauty and excellence support one another, and they are both supported by the Truth of Who We Really Are.

K. **Fairness, equity and justice:** Fairness is very simply our ability to live by the golden rule. Are we treating others the way we want to be treated? Are we doing to others as we would have them do unto us? Equity and Justice are our ability to operate with fairness as a value in each moment, be it with ourselves, another person, or within a group, institution or community. This strength is about living a life in balance and respect for ourselves and those around us.

L. **Gratitude:** Gratitude is the art of acknowledging the many gifts all around us and within us in each and every moment. The practice of gratitude is one of the strongest actions we can take in creating a more positive and productive mindset. When we can connect with even one thing that we are grateful for, we are connecting with the Goodness in our world, and opening the door to Hope for that Goodness to blossom in our lives in all the ways we want and need.

"HONESTY STARTS WITH AN HONEST CONVERSATION WITHIN OURSELVES.

M. **Social intelligence:** We are very intelligent people, and there are many ways for us to tap into our intelligence. Some people are very good at learning new languages. Others are great at learning how to play sports. Still others are great at picking up musical instruments and playing something melodic. *Intelligence comes in many shapes and sizes.* Social intelligence is our ability to navigate the social interactions of our lives with grace and ease. It is our ability to read other people, and situations involving them, and act in a way that brings us to our desired outcome. Social intelligence requires a great deal of self-awareness, perspective, empathy, and attention. This is a high-level skill requiring a true sense of presence in the moment.

N. **Caution, prudence and discretion:** When we walk slowly, mindfully, and with awareness, we are walking with an eye to what is the best next step. We direct our journey and land ourselves exactly where we need to be. Caution is the ability to look with a sense of safety and protection to what lies ahead. It is a healthy way to interact with new people, places and experiences. Prudence is our ability to go slow before we go fast. We can take small steps, mindful risks, and move in a way that allows trust to build organically. Discretion is the art of sharing information with caution and an eye to prudence. These strengths allow us to show up with integrity and mindfulness, and *walk our paths wisely.*

Case Study

Bobby was the CEO of a multi-billion dollar hedge fund on Madison Avenue. His job, all day, every day, was to connect with the right people and keep growing the fund. At the heart of his role was social intelligence, his ability to navigate social interactions with professionalism and an eye for new opportunities for the other person and his company. I remember going to lunch with Bobby one day at a very ritzy sushi place in the heart of mid-town Manhattan. We were casually discussing communication skills, and we began chatting about Active-Constructive Listening and Responding. He had never heard the term before, and his eyes lit up as we began to get into the content. The gold standard of any type of productive conversation is respectful presence and acknowledgement. When we actively listen, we are truly taking in what the other person in saying. We are being present with them. When we actively respond, we are acknowledging what they have shared and offer something of value in return. When we show up with respectful intention and a presence of mind, we are actively constructing a positive relationship. Bobby took this forward with him and continues to lead major corporations to positive outcomes.

O. Humour and playfulness: We all have an inner child, and very often, that inner child wants to play! When we tap into our playful nature, we are able to enjoy our lives in the moment. In Buddhism there is something called the beginners mind, which is simply a sense of looking at life without judgment, as if we are seeing something for the first time. Playfulness allows us to step into a place of joyful flow, letting go of the paradigms of judging unnecessarily. Humour is playfulness in action. When we can laugh with our lives, when we can find levity in our ups and downs, when we can giggle in the face of challenge, we are able to approach the needs of each day with a buoyant step and a lightness of being. Humour and playfulness just may be a direct door to our connection with a power greater than ourselves.

P. Perspective (wisdom): Perspective is the ability to see something from various vantage points, to take a variety of points of view and look through a variety of lenses as we navigate the Universe. This may be challenging for us as we often like to look through our sense of self. Often what a wider sense of wisdom requires is the ability to put ourselves aside and look through a lens of empathy, compassion and kindness. Perspective requires us to show up with an open mind, and often an open heart. When we are able to do this, we just may be able to see what is in front of us.

Q. Capacity to love and be loved: Though this may seem straightforward enough, this may be the most difficult strength to master for many of us. The capacity to love and be loved begins with our ability to love with ourselves. Love is hard to define, but may be generally known as the goodness, kindness, compassion and care expressed and experienced internally and between people. Love may extend into spiritual practices and connections as well. Some theorise that love as energy is a fabric that connects all life, and perhaps the entire known Universe. Our capacity to love and to be loved is really our capacity to tap into the goodness present within us and around us, and to share it with ourselves and others.

R. Bravery and valour: The world is full of challenges. Life takes bravery, a sense of courage and strength, to step up to these challenges as they show up. Valour is that internal sense of character that allows us to express the bravery within us. We all have tremendous bravery within us, and it is often when we are tested that we realize just how very brave we are. *This strength is all about showing up.*

S. Kindness and generosity: "If you want other people to be happy, practice compassion. If you want to be happy, practice compassion." - Dalai Lama. Kindness is compassion in action. When we are generous with our energy, we are connecting with, and contributing to, the goodness of the global community. When we help others, when we are kind, we are supporting the greatest good of all.

T. Modesty and humility: When we see the grand scheme of things, modesty and humility are easy. This world is vast and there are incredible people everywhere. Modesty is our ability to honour our strengths and the strengths of others. Humility is our ability to stay grounded even when we excel, to see our accomplishments and not let our egos take over. When we can stay modest and humble, we are able to stay connected to God.

U. Leadership: Leading is teaching. It is really that simple. Teaching a vision, a story, a way of being or a skill. Leadership requires a number of other strengths, such as social intelligence, bravery, capacity to love and be loved, modesty and self-regulation. When we lead, we are actively being of service. Leadership is nothing short of an art.

V. Spirituality, sense of purpose and faith: Spirituality is our experience of something greater than ourselves. Faith is our trust in that. Sense of purpose is born out of committing our lives to a mission, vision, cause or group that shows us something we deem right, just and of value, perhaps even a calling. This strength unites all other strengths within us. As we connect with our sense of purpose, faith and spirituality, we are connecting with our authentic selves, and the authentic selves of those in our lives. It is through this authenticity that we can truly know love, and truly perform at our peak. *In a way, Peak Performance is a Spiritual Practice, and one guided by a Love for Who We Are and What We Do.*

W. Love of learning: We are all learning more every day. Life is a process of learning. Our world is our classroom. We can embrace this truth, or we can reject it. When we embrace it fully, and take life as an opportunity for our soul's to learn on a diverse and rich canvas, we are embracing our love of learning. When we love the process, the process just may love us back.

X. Self-control and self-regulation: For many of us, self-control and self-regulation may be the most challenging strengths of all. Self-control is the ability to make choices beyond instincts, drives and desires. To weigh our options and choose wisely with our minds, bodies and spirits in harmony. Self-regulation is the ability to keep that harmony going. This strength is all about conscious connection, awareness, mindful living and the strength to act in such a way that best supports our own well-being, and the well being of those around us.

MIND – THE BIGGEST ASSET

"THE FIRST STEP IN DETERMINING YOUR TRUE POTENTIAL IS TO REALIZE THAT EXTERNAL CIRCUMSTANCES, SUCH AS PHYSICAL, ENVIRONMENTAL LIMITATIONS, AND FINANCIAL CONSTRAINTS DO NOT HAVE ANY IMPACT ON REACHING THE SUCCESS. THE ONLY COMMON ASPECT AND AN IMPORTANT ASSET IS THE MIND."

– KUSAL

If you are in a position to unlock your mind, you have gained the maximum potential that your system can achieve in this world. By unlocking the potential, overcoming fears and failures is possible. You will no longer limit yourself to social phobias. You will discover the gifts and the talents that you possess and gain an insight into their development. You will be in a position to spot the new opportunities and learn the necessary skills that support personal development.

Unlocking the potential will give you the strength and the sense of purpose. You will begin to value your life in this world and create a difference by returning your talents. You will gain the passion for learning, to develop, and to create challenges in an enthusiastic way. You will be in a situation to conquer any challenge in your life and move towards it in a fun way. You will no longer feel the stress, burden, or fear of a challenge. You will gain complete control over your senses, giving you the ability to have a balanced life.

CREATING PASSION AND PURPOSE- 6 TIPS FROM KUSAL

We are different from each other and have a different path to walk in this world. It is necessary to find the object and the passion for leading a happy life. However, if you have ever felt that you had something to give to the world and were unsure about it, the following ideas will help you out in unlocking the mystery.

1. Fears

Learning to overcome fears is an essential aspect. What you fear may be the one thing that keeps you away from success. It may also be your destiny. Begin with writing down your fears and the negative feelings towards them. You will then find the possible reasons and the exact opposite solutions. For instance, if you possess a fear of public speaking but love to share ideas and thoughts, you may consider the role of the writer. You can bring out your talent through the form of words.

2. Fear of failing

It is natural for any person to avoid something that they are sure of failing. Nevertheless, these are the only things that we want the most. Explore all your fears and write down when you have avoided something or said something because you are scared. You will probably find your answer.

3. Energy

Apart from self-motivation, external energy drives us towards our goal. This energy comes from people surrounded in your life. Make sure you are in a group of people that align with a similar mindset. Mingle with people who are full of life and enthusiasm. It will affect your passion and the zeal to unleash the potential that you possess. All you have to do is explore people and learn it through experience.

4. Time frame

It is frustrating for any individual when they can clearly see where they want to reach in life. However, reaching the destination is not the only aspect of life. You will have to begin by breaking the target into manageable chunks. Set realistic goals to achieve the step comfortability. Take a moment to enjoy the achievement, as it will improve self-confidence and boost morale. Try to be patient and learn to prepare a course of action to reach faster.

5. Current status

It is necessary to evaluate your status and position, before beginning the journey. You will have to accept who you are as a person and understand your limitations. Irrespective of the circumstances and external conditions, the status in which you live today is because you choose to be there. It is because of your past and the decisions that you have taken.

Accept yourself and love yourself. It is a valuable tool in moving ahead and overcome any circumstance from tomorrow.

6. Others

You are a unique body and have a unique fashion. You do not have to worry about other people and treat their passion as yours. Although the elements are the same, majority are custom fit. Stop comparing your passion with others. You will only move towards a negative direction, when you begin comparing yourself and your passions with the rest of the people. Try to understand the fact that you have your ability and skill set that is different from others. Additionally, the approach you intend to make is quite different, and no one else can make it. *Begin with accepting yourself and loving yourself.* Do not ever compare with others. When you do, you start to make negative judgments, which leads to the development of fear.

TRY TO UNDERSTAND THE FACT THAT YOU HAVE YOUR ABILITY AND SKILL SET THAT IS DIFFERENT FROM OTHERS.

The Hierarchy of Commitment

Level of Commitment

Commitment	I Will Do It! I Will Lead Others To Do It...
Compliance	I Have to Do It! I Can Do It When I am Told To...
Complain	Why Should I Do It? If Nobody Say So...
Non-Committal/Condemn	I Will Not Do It! I Will Influence Others...

COMMITMENT

Once you understand your potential and the purpose, *write it down*. Make sure to keep it simple and clear. Break the purpose into sizeable chunks. For instance, if you plan to become a research analyst, write down the steps necessary to achieve that. It includes the requirement of the qualifications, the ability required in understanding analysis, and certificate courses that support your studies. **These possibilities act as mini goals.** Reach each mini goal with preparation. This way, you will ultimately reach the final step of the purpose.

Make sure to write down the vision and read it aloud every night and morning. It will help in preparing your mind and questioning the motives to reach the goals. Once you receive the answers to the possible questions, you will find yourself confident and the energy to complete the task. **It is necessary for you to begin loving yourself before you can start focusing on the target.** You cannot demand someone else to love you until you love yourself. Make sure to remind of the purpose that you have created and its importance.

Read books that motivate you, listen, and watch things that motivate you. Try to keep away from people who often let you down. Stimulate each other by participating in a group of people that are full of life and enthusiasm.

The ability to become successful and reach the purpose is a direct proportion to the control of your mind. It is important for you to **unlock the potential of your mind** and control your thought process. You will start believing in yourself as soon as you open the door, which you have closed for a long time.

According to Princeton and Stanford Universities research, people possess the ability to alter or influence the thoughts of others. Although the research had a significant impact on the effects of random statistical experimentation using number generation and rolling dice, there is a scientific belief that it is possible to change the course of actions by your thoughts. Although there is no anecdotal evidence, you can judge for yourself by your actions and the outcomes.

Even in a worst-case scenario, a positive approach is likely to help you come out of

Hannah, who started treatment for her cerebral palsy before her 10th birthday, was afflicted by this from birth. Walking, talking and writing all needed some form of assistance. Due to this she had a full time carer. Her life ambition was to be a doctor. The physiotherapy team worked with her for 5 years. She never complained, she never made any excuses, she always attended her physiotherapy rehabilitation sessions and she kept to the plan to execute her life goal. She is in her early twenties now and she is well on her way to being a doctor. This has been attributed to 2 major factors - love from her family and a long term plan with exercises (physiotherapy) speech rehabilitation (speech pathology) and writing improvement (occupational therapy). Her number one requirement over the years was her strong mindset. Having this mental strength has allowed her to stick to the long term plan, through the ups and downs.

the situation by searching an opportunity. Such an approach paves the path for opening up new ideas and tools. You now possess the ability to turn your life the way you want it to be. All you must do is discover yourself and the purpose that you were born to live. Remember that the place you are in now is because of your decisions and thoughts. You do have the power to change it and become successful by aligning to the positive direction of life. Start taking over the future by bringing your conscious and subconscious minds together. Learn to turn around any situation by using your thoughts.

Once you gain the ability to address small issues and build a stronger mind, you will soon reach the aims that you have placed in your life. All you have to do is begin your day with a positive attitude and continue it until the end. Mingle with people and move in surroundings that help you and boost your confidence and morale.

ALL YOU MUST DO IS DISCOVER YOURSELF AND THE PURPOSE THAT YOU WERE BORN TO LIVE.

CHAPTER 4

SAYING NO TO OLD SCHOOL TECHNIQUES

JUMP IN THE DEEP END- WHO HAS TIME FOR THAT?

Many people think that in order to start a meditation practice, or to make any healthy lifestyle change, they need to jump in the deep end, apply an all or nothing mentality, and do it now. This might work for some people and some changes, but if you are like most people I've worked with, *the best changes take time, practice, commitment and a slow and steady learning curve.*

When beginning a Peak Performance Mindset Thinking exercise, we might be so used to focusing on the negative that we find it hard to think about how to take a small step. Similarly, when we try to quiet the mind, breathe and rest in a meditative space that feeling of "go-go-go, Do-do-do" may be overwhelming and can make even one minute of quiet meditation feel like an eternity.

The bottom line here is that jumping in the deep end may not be realistic and likely will not create lasting results. Even if you can sit in quiet meditation for 10 days straight, will that become a daily practice that feels good to you for the rest of your life? Even if you can force yourself to think positively for a full day, will that mean that you begin to naturally go to a place of positive thinking, solution focus and optimism when crisis hits?

Jumping in the deep end may seem like a good idea, but after a while, what first felt invigorating can feel like a burden, and it is essential that we Enjoy The Process In Order For Meaningful, Lasting Change To Occur.

I. BITING OFF A LOT AT ONCE- REALISTIC GOAL SETTING THEORY

So when we think about jumping in the deep end, we can similarly think about biting off a lot at once. Let's say your goal is to lose five pounds of fat and increase your feelings of overall well-being, happiness and tranquillity by 25%. These can be very realistic goals depending upon the timeline we set.

Snyder and Lopez, two leading researchers in the field of positive psychology, looked at the styles of goal setting that support positive outcomes. The results they came up with may seem obvious, but somehow we often do not follow this rationale. If we make a goal too small, say to lose 1 lb and increase feelings of well-being by 1% in the next month, our work may be hard to measure and the benefits may not give us much of a positive reward or feeling of satisfaction, and we may actually become less likely to achieve our goals! Even if they are super achievable!

If we set our goals too high, saying that we want to lose 20 lbs and increase happiness by 200% in the next month, then we are setting ourselves up for burnout and a sense of failure.

"IF, HOWEVER, WE SET OUR GOALS TO A REALISTIC AMOUNT AND ON A REALISTIC TIMELINE, WE ARE SETTING OURSELVES UP FOR SUCCESS."

– HELENE

We can look at what experts say about our particular desired changes, our history on a project or behavioural change, and come up with a realistic and challenging goal. When we have a harmony of skill, challenge and passion, we might even find a place of flow in our goal-achievement endeavours. (For more on flow see Mihalyi Chikszentmihalyi's research.)

The long and short of it here is that we want to challenge ourselves, but not too much. We want to push ourselves, but not too far. **We want to keep striving, but in a way that feels healthy and happy each step of the way.** We want to set up goals we can achieve. We want to set up track-records of success. We want to look back with integrity and say to ourselves, "I said I would do it, and I did."

"I ONCE HAD A MENTOR WHO SUGGESTED THAT I GO LIVE IN INDIA AT AN ASHRAM FOR A COUPLE OF YEARS BEFORE GOING OUT IN THE WORLD AND TEACHING MEDITATION. HE WAS A GREAT MENTOR, BUT THAT WAS ONE SUGGESTION I COULD NOT AGREE WITH."

– HELENE

II. SITTING ON A MOUNTAIN TOP- MEDITATION FOR BUSY PEOPLE

My path has been one of many different types of meditation commitments. Some days it is simply one deep breath, other days I have spent most of my waking hours in meditation. Sometimes my meditations are quiet. Other times my meditations happen in front of a Funktion One sound system with music that shakes the concrete floor.

WE WANT TO PUSH OURSELVES, BUT NOT TOO FAR.

"MEDITATION
COMES IN
MANY SHAPES
AND SIZES, JUST
LIKE US."

– HELENE

In my experience, we do not need to sit on a mountain top or live in a foreign country for years in order to achieve a sense of connection and inner peace. We are busy people living busy lives. We are movers and shakers, innovators and doers, and though we may need to reign in those tendencies when we get too caught up, there is also a real beauty in that desire to create, that drive to achieve, that ambition to be at the top of our game.

Meditation is neither better nor worse if it is a short practice or a full-days commitment. And meditation is neither better nor worse if it is done in an Ashram, a Temple, a Church, or a Warehouse.

Meditation is about creating a practice of tuning into ourselves, and in doing so, connecting with the loving energy beyond ourselves that connects us throughout the Universe. Meditation is an access point to understanding that little word called 'God' and what in the world it might actually mean.

For busy people like us, we need systems that work in our lifestyles.

Consistency is the key and showing up is half the battle.

It is not about how long we are in our practice; it is about our ability to show up for it, for ourselves, and for our loved ones in the first place. The rest is the path. The rest is the journey. We stand here, at the doorstep of a new way. Are you prepared to take just that one first step?

III. LAW OF ATTRACTION IS ALL YOU NEED - INCOMPLETE STARTING POINT, NEED FOR HEALTHY HABITS AND DAILY PRACTICE FOR POSITIVE THINKING STYLES AND BEHAVIOURS TO MATCH!

There has been a lot of talk about something called **The Law of Attraction.** Very simply put, this is the idea that our thoughts create reality, and if we want something, we need to visualize it and think of it as already here. The flip side of this law states that if we are worried, concerned and frightened, the universe cannot tell the difference and, thus, we might manifest what we do not want if we focus on it too much.

Now, I don't know about you, but not once have I ever seen a monster appear under my bed. The fear or hope that simply thinking about something will make it suddenly appear is just plain unrealistic. We can send ourselves into panic attacks taking on too much of an omnipotent world view, assuming we are creating every bit of reality by our thoughts alone.

Yes, thoughts matter. And Yes, thinking in a certain way will help us move towards desired outcomes. But thoughts themselves are not enough. We need ACTION.

Our behaviours, our habits and our daily action items are the vehicle through which manifestation occurs. We create what we envision and work towards, and we co-create with others who are working with us towards a shared vision.

> "IF OUR THOUGHTS AND BEHAVIOURS ARE NOT ALIGNED, WE ARE UNLIKELY TO SEE RESULTS."
>
> – HELENE

Old school methods are no longer the realm. We are far ahead and possess proven methods that truly help in building self-confidence, determination, and the zeal to complete a task. The same is applicable to your exercise regimen.

The old-school believed in achieving things by pushing the body through pain. Of course, to some point, it is a reality, but it no longer stands as the standard equation that you have to follow. The old-school laid those principles according to their age, environment and the necessity. Nevertheless, today we live in a better world with advanced technology.

Many people experience niggling pain that makes it impossible to have a comfortable exercise regimen. There is no denying that exercising causes discomfort in the beginning. It can even hurt. However, stopping the activities at the first sign of the workout will probably halt the task that you took up to reduce weight. It will in turn lower your self-confidence and the enthusiasm that you wished to pose to achieve success and overcome challenges in the daily life.

It is essential to understand the difference between pain and discomfort, before beginning any exercises. According to physiologists, discomfort and effort, often go hand-in-hand and is the sign of the good pain. However, you tend to feel a small degree of discomfort. Continuing the exercise will lead to the development of actual pain that may be stabbing, burning or sharp. It is not a good sign, and you should stop the exercise immediately.

IT IS ESSENTIAL TO UNDERSTAND THE DIFFERENCE BETWEEN PAIN AND DISCOMFORT.

According to researchers, it is common for an individual to feel discomfort from fatigue during exercises. However, acute pain associated with injury or illness, is not. If there is a joint or musculoskeletal pain, you should stop the activity immediately. The indication of the pain resembles the excessive amount of pressure that the entire body is undergoing.

In order to understand the difference, the best method is just to stop the exercise. So when you experience a little burn in the muscles, stop participating in the exercise immediately. If the burn disappears after a few minutes, it is okay to continue the exercise. The burning sensation appears, as it is the result of the exercise. It is common and assists in burning unwanted calories in the body. However, if the pain reappears when you continue, such as a sharp pain in the knees or a painful twinge in the hamstring, then you have likely overdone the exercise. It's time to stop. Learning such differentiating methods will help you to reduce the burden that you might be causing on your body due to exercise.

One of the most common discomforts while performing strenuous exercise is the burning sensation in the muscles or lungs. It usually passes after you stop the activity. The discomfort is because of the build-up of lactic acid. It is also responsible for causing the burning sensation during jogging or during exercises where you lift weights.

The body releases lactic acid, which is a by-product when the body produces more energy than needed. This can happen when over-exercising. The body needs to produce energy at a faster rate so you can continue to perform the strenuous exercise. Usually, the muscular structure utilizes energy aerobically with oxygen. However, when you over-perform an exercise, there is a reduction in that oxygen supply. At this point of time, the muscular structure generates energy anaerobically. Lactic acid is the by-product of that process. The harder you work and push your limit, the bigger the build up of lactic acid in the body. Nevertheless, the cleaning of the lactic acid depends upon your body's fitness. Consistent exercising will help you attain endurance and fitness. It is at this point of time that the body has the ability to clear the build up of lactic acid.

It is normal for athletes to thrust themselves out of their comfort zone. However, if you begin to experience pain when you push yourself outside the comfort zone, it is better to stop exercising and seek the assistance of a qualified physical trainer. Physical trainers will teach the necessary actions you should follow while exercising. They will also teach you the number of repetitions that best suits your physical fitness level. You will probably increase repetitions gradually but you will be attaining the fitness and endurance necessary to slowly push the limits.

> # "PHYSICAL EXERCISES BEGIN WITH THE SIMPLEST FORM OF ACTIVITIES."
>
> **– KUSAL**

This ensures the body receives flexibility and endurance before moving towards more complex activities. Any physical trainer should teach flexibility exercises in the beginning. You will be performing those activities until you find yourself comfortable with the movements. Once you achieve this state, you will now move towards the medium exercises where you have to exert pressure on the musculoskeletal structure. The gradual increase ensures there is no stress on muscles, ligaments, and tissues.

Apart from the exercises, you will have to keep an eye on the foods that you consume. Keep away from high-calorie foods. They only increase the fat content and make it difficult for you to shed them in the later stages. Additionally, consumption of high-calorie food increases laziness, which stops you from performing your regular activities with enthusiasm.

Old school techniques are no longer the standards to achieve good health. The availability of technology has made it possible for physical trainers and doctors to address critical factors supporting fitness in a good way. The threshold for pain doesn't exist. It isn't set and it changes as you progress. However, limitation of the pressure that you can put on your total system does exist.

The initial steps of physical exercises concentrate on posture, stability, and balance. Along with these, you will also learn to gain control over your breathing. It is common for breathing to go overboard as soon as you begin the exercise. However, learning to regulate breathing has a positive impact on your health. Your physical trainer can provide tips and assurance.

"DON'T LOOK AT EXERCISE AS A RACE. YOU DON'T HAVE TO JOIN A CLASS TO BECOME AN ATHLETE. YOU HAVE TO UNDERSTAND THAT EXERCISES HELP IMPROVE YOUR HEALTH – INTERNALLY AND EXTERNALLY. IT GIVES YOU THE CHANCE TO ENHANCE YOUR MOOD AND GAIN THE POWER TO UNLEASH YOUR POTENTIAL. OPENING NEW DOORS AND IMPROVING BRAIN ACTIVITY RESULTS IN POSITIVE ATTITUDE GROWTH, WHICH HAS A SIGNIFICANT IMPACT ON YOUR THOUGHT PROCESS. YOU WILL BE IN A STATE TO DEAL WITH SEVERAL CHALLENGES AND OVERCOME THEM WITHOUT STRESS."

– KUSAL

Another interesting concept is diet. Of course, diet is an excellent way to build good health. Diet plans focus on increasing fruits and vegetables and eliminating processed foods. However, the focus should not be just to lose weight quickly. Instead, losing weight in a healthy way is necessary. **You should not have a set period in which to lose weight.** The essential element of the task is to lose weight in a healthy way.

Fad diets have become common. However, they pose a threat to your health. You should be strictly against choosing a fad diet; they lead to dehydration, constipation, nausea, weakness, and fatigue. Making the body weak causes stress on the nervous system and organs. They work harder to support the system, and in some cases they over-work. Since your body doesn't receive its share of energy, your organs consume and work on the available resources within your body. This leads to health ailments and medical conditions.

You have a unique physical structure and internal system. **It's vital that you design a diet and exercise regimen that suits to your health.** You shouldn't considering any programs that are available on the Internet. They are too general, so can have a varying effect on individuals. It is preferable to consult a dietician and physiotherapist to receive proper guidance. They prepare a tailor-made session suitable to your level of fitness. You can perform the activity at your pace. But remember to follow the schedule! Don't skip an activity. Doing so will affect your confidence and bring it down further.

Participate actively and follow your diet to receive the **maximum health benefits.** You will be happy to see the outcomes within a short time. Regular participation improves your morale and helps build a stronger mind.

Henry had suffered from back pain for 20 years. Over the years he had all treatments under the sun – manual treatment, acupuncture, naturopathy, eastern medicine, western medicine, scans, blood tests, internal organ tests and even brain scans. Nothing got him results. He approached us due to Elite Akademy's adage, 'we make a difference in 3 sessions or less'. Within the first 2 sessions a neural tension issue was identified. Once this was done he responded quickly to more manual sports physiotherapy treatment. Within 12 weeks he had improved by 50% and within 24 weeks he had improved to 75%. In over 20 years he had spent close to $100,000 in medical expenses. He has now improved by 85% and only spent just over $4500 to achieve his results. Why the difference? Go to health professional who are objective in their results. Go to those who can make a difference in three sessions or less. There is a big difference between 'healing in three sessions' versus 'making a difference in three sessions or less'. If Henry didn't get results or we couldn't make a difference within three sessions then he would have been referred to an appropriate specialist who would follow the same guidelines. This ensures that a person's problems are solved through focus, objective results and clear communication.

YOU SHOULD BE STRICTLY AGAINST CHOOSING A FAD DIET: THEY LEAD TO DEHYDRATION, CONSTIPATION, NAUSEA, WEAKNESS, AND FATIGUE.

CHAPTER 5

SOLUTIONS FOR THE MODERN WORLD

lenty of resolutions are available for you to transform your life and make it successful. Have you ever considered introducing a new habit into your life? You may have given up a new habit because you couldn't get used to the new activity. Perhaps the excitement of doing something new gave way to a new pressure on your daily life, and took so much from it that you couldn't perform it through to the end. Perhaps attempting to complete the task eventually became a low priority. When urgency precedes importance, people forget their resolutions unfortunately.

Irrespective of the actions, in the end, you couldn't complete the work. You will only transform your life and the decisions that you choose based on your daily life. The 21-day program is an attractive tool that gives you the ability to introduce new habits into your daily lives. The self-initiated program concentrates on continuing a particular activity for a period of 21 days. Although the program focuses on improving the good habits, you have the freedom to include new practices and try out new ideas that would facilitate good health and life. Additional activities include exercising, quitting unprocessed food, sticking to a particular diet, reading a book, meditating, quitting alcohol, and smoking, making new friends, and valuing time. The list is endless, and you have the freedom to create your list based on your requirement.

The 21-day program allows you to cultivate good habits. It is also useful in breaking bad habits. All you should do is prepare a course of action based on the list of habits that you would like to cultivate. Begin by choosing the most important of all, and then proceed towards its implementation. For example, if you intend to reduce weight and follow a specific diet, begin the program by taking the necessary steps. Prepare the schedule and follow it for the next 21 days without skipping a single day.

The 21-day program is a useful improvement tool as it helps you to build success in your life. Furthermore, you will also improve the quality of life and fill it with happiness and valuable memories.

YOU WILL ONLY TRANSFORM YOUR LIFE AND THE DECISIONS THAT YOU CHOOSE BASED ON YOUR DAILY LIFE.

Extensive research and studies show that it takes 21 days for a person to introduce a new habit or succeed in eliminating a bad habit. The research indicates that it takes 21 days for the neuropathways to develop and get used to the new habit. Therefore, continuing your particular activity continuously for a period of 21 days instils the necessary pathway in the brain, which helps you perform the action for the rest of the life. You will notice this is your self-evaluation.

Furthermore, the 21-day program is a more efficient process than a 30-day period. That's because you get used to the new habit in a shorter time. You will also find time to evaluate the past 21 days and draw the necessary conclusions. Self-evaluation gives you the ability to boost your self-confidence and moral. It will help you move ahead and incorporate other habits on your list.

BENEFITS

1. Easy management

Unlike a stricter regimen, the 21-day program gives you freedom and flexibility. Many people delay the implementation of things that they would like to do, such as good habits, and this has a significant impact on their lives. A critical reason for this procrastination is the thought that they have to do the new habit or activity for the rest of their life. People begin thinking in a negative way and try to avoid it as much as possible. On the other hand, the 21-day program is a time-based assessment. You have to perform an activity or indulge in the habit for just 21 days. It's a short period, and you can easily complete the activity with ease. There will be no more excuses, and you can channel your efforts and introduce a new habit into your life by participating actively for just three weeks. Before you know it, it is all behind you, and in the past!

2. No commitment

As the 21-day program allows you to evaluate the effect of a new habit or an activity in your life, you do not have to commit yourself to the program. The self-evaluation procedure gives you a better idea whether the new habit has a positive or negative effect on your daily life. Based on the result, you can make a final decision whether to continue or select another habit that truly transforms your life.

The highly manageable and non-committal structure of the program gives rise to the following benefits.

a. People have a lot of good things that they would like to cultivate and introduce into their life. This includes exercising, avoiding unhealthy food, developing positive attitude, and so on. Although they make a mental note to introduce it into their life, they never concentrate on it because of several reasons.

Rather than waste time and energy in thinking about wanting to do it, the 21-day program acts as a foundation to introduce the good habits. For example, you might have thought about getting up early every day for the past year. However, you never gave a shot at it. With the help of the 21-day program, you can include it in your daily life and evaluate whether getting up early, was useful to your life or not. Such small instances contribute significantly to improving the quality and health of life.

b. The 21-day program also acts as an experimental ground. You have the opportunity to try out new things. We have several things that we would like to do in our lifetime. However, we may give up our desires and lead a mechanical life to survive in the world.

You often declare an activity or a habit as unfeasible before trying it or experiencing. Such a mindset will leave you behind in this wonderful world of ours. You may not be able to test your limits and understand the potential. With the help of 21-day program, you can easily implement it and verify whether the action has positive or negative effect. The primary aim of the program is the ability that it gives you to experience several things for yourself. *You do not have to depend on other people's reviews and debates.* The 21-day program is an excellent opportunity to introduce all the good habits that you wanted to cultivate in your life. It acts as a training ground, where you develop concentration, skills, self-discipline, and motivation. It is a fun way to try new things and learn about your boundaries and limits.

TERMS OF THE 21-DAY PROGRAM

The only condition for effective results in the 21-day program is to perform the activity continuously for 21 days. You should not miss even a single day. Remember that you have to begin the action from the start. There are no exceptions. Breaking the routine even a single day will affect the overall experience of the activity as well as the ability to develop the neuropathways that will assist with the addition of the new habit. Successful completion of the program enables you to rectify and evaluate the process. The evaluation gives you the possibility to proceed with the habit or choose another habit.

IT TAKES 21 DAYS FOR A PERSON TO INTRODUCE A NEW HABIT OR SUCCEED IN ELIMINATING A BAD HABIT.

6 STRATEGY KEYS FOR SUCCESSFUL OUTCOMES
FROM KUSAL

1. Research

Carrying out research is an essential element that will help you prepare for the habit. Research also gives you the chance to understand the process that you must implement for the next 21 days. You will also learn about the problems that others faced during the program. This information will help you prepare a strategy that reduces the barriers and provides the chance to excel.

2. Trial

Try the habit in a general way for a few days, before beginning the 21-day program. It acts as a test and helps you in understanding the procedures that you are required to follow. You will be prepared ahead for the 21-day program in order to complete it with ease.

3. Mental preparation

Preparing mentally before the activity has its advantages. You will put yourself in the right mood and move towards success. During this period, you can choose to implement the activity in a smaller magnitude. You will then be able to create the momentum necessary to go ahead with the actual 21-day program.

4. Tracking

Tracking the progress has a big effect on the program. It's crucial that you to record all the things that you are doing during the 21-day program. Make sure to read it at least once a day. Make sure that it is visible in an appropriate place. It will remind you always of your new obligation. You can cross out a day as soon as you complete it. It will give you a sense of gratification for the hard work that you put in to complete that single day in the overall 21-day program. You will slowly build the confidence to move ahead with the rest of the program and complete it, as planned.

5. One at a time

Take each step at a time. Make sure that you do not clump everything into the 21-day program. Remember that you are introducing the habit into the daily life by making a few changes. Furthermore, you have other activities in your life that you have to attend. Divide the goal into small chunks so that you can easily complete them within the stipulated time. If you are capable of handling multiple activities at a single time, ensure that you can club two or more habits into a unique program.

6. Affirmations

Write down affirmations in a positive tense before beginning the activity. Write down the activity in the present-tense. For example, write down "I am happy today" rather than "I will be happy today". The former sentence sends a signal to the subconscious mind that the activity has already been implemented and successful. Through this process, you will be ready to overcome the barrier that most people feel during the first few days of the program.

EXPECTATIONS FROM THE PROGRAM

Week 1: Induction

The first week of the curriculum consists of introducing the habit into the daily life. In order to complete it fast and without any trouble, you have to build the momentum that lets you perform it with ease.

Week 2: Resistance

The second week is of utmost important. You will experience a number of resistances in different variants, which all act towards lowering your motivation towards the challenge. As you have prepared yourself mentally before beginning the program, you will easily overcome the situation and complete the task with ease.

Week 3: Integration

The third week is the level where the habit becomes a part of your life. Although you have completed two weeks since the beginning of introducing the habit, it seems distant when you reach the third week. However, if you have already prepared the strategy and the action plan, you may be wondering why it needed so long to complete the task. It becomes so easy that you wonder why you could not do it before. You will have a better imagination of the things that you can do. Instantly, there is an increase in self-confidence and a quick boost to your morale. The lift will give you the possibility to implement other habits with ease.

EXERCISE DIARY

An Exercise Diary is a roadmap and a handy tool that helps you evaluate and analyze the progress. An exercise diary is where you will find all the details necessary before beginning an exercise program and a diet chart. In a number of ways, the diary is informative. It records the journey of your training program and the progress that you are making towards the fitness goal.

Statistical data shows that every two out of three people are either overweight or obese. If you are in either of these categories, it's necessary to reduce calorie-intake to improve your health. Maintaining the exercise diary will help you record the daily activities of the program. It further develops a habit and ensures that you continue the program until the end. In the end, you will receive benefits and experience a change in your life. You will gain a positive attitude, an increase in self-confidence, and the ability to overcome any challenge that comes your way.

Several online exercise diaries also provide information about activities that consume higher calories. The journal will provide you information about the start date along with time consumed for the activity. You can further include the trained body parts for a session. The diary also gives you the chance to record information about the cardiovascular activities. It forms the basis of the exercise and gives you details about a particular session's progress.

If weight training is in your exercise regimen, it is important that you record the quantity of reps and sets that you finish in a session. Furthermore, you will also obtain the ability to record details about the warm up sets. The availability of such features gives you an insight into the progress before the beginning of the session. Through this, you will be in a position to avoid injuries and reduce the warm up sets to suit according to your body.

With the help of the exercise diary, you will be able to **calculate the total amount of calorie intake and physical activities.** The details give you the opportunity to carry out the analysis and check whether you are meeting the required levels or not. The presence of the technology has made it possible to introduce online exercise diaries that maintain the entire record of accomplishment. In addition, they also calculate the calorie intake based on the input and display the result. You no longer must go through the tiresome charts and jump across rows and columns to record data.

In addition to the quantity of sets and reps, you will also have the possibility to record the weight utilized for lift during this session. It would be difficult for you to remember the exact amount of weight, when you perform a series of activities in a section. **With the help of the exercise diary, you will be in a position to record and eliminate the guesswork.**

You can also indicate whether you are using any special training techniques such as negatives, elements, forced reps or supersets. You will be able to analyze whether any of

EXERCISES AND DIET HAVE AN IMMENSE IMPACT ON THE OUTCOME.

the training technique had a positive effect on your health. You will also understand whether the technique is a burden or you are comfortable in completing the set. You can even record the use of the machines, adjustments to it, and the seating arrangement. All these actions will create a routine and save you plenty of time for the next session.

Details of an exercise have an immense impact on the overall result. With the help of the exercise diary, you can easily record the feelings and the details related to a particular activity. Recording the feelings during the activity enables you to fix any mistakes or utilize the advantages during the next session to receive an even higher benefit. For example, playing your favourite music will substantially affect the success of your workout. *If you feel better you will perform better. This will lead to results.*

Exercises and diet have an immense impact on the outcome. Apart from recording the activities of the exercises, it is also crucial to note down about your diet. Diet plays a vital role in expanding your energy development and supports the exercise regimen. It ensures that the body receives the right amount of nutrients in appropriate proportions. Recording the food that you consume provides you a better idea about the body.

It is also imperative to measure vital stats. It helps you understand about the progress that you are displaying. By keeping a track of the measurements, moving towards the goal becomes easy. You can take measurements of your neck, upper arms, chest, waist, calves, and thighs. The details provide you with enhanced information about your training progress. You will also remain motivated and continue with the program.

The exercise diary records every action of your daily activity. You can refer to the details before proceeding with the next session. Going through the details and measurements helps you to move closer towards your goal. With plenty of information available at hand, you can probably increase the reps or add weight. You can boost your morale to push the limits and test your potential.

The exercise book is of huge importance. With every detail recorded in it, you will have the best details you need to carry out a thorough analysis. You will be ready to focus on the areas that you have not concentrated on before and design a new program. It is also the best time to look at the correlation between the training session and physical changes. Furthermore, the nutritional record keeps you informed about the foods that had a significant effect on the entire regimen. You can always get back to the right food and maintain a healthy diet that improves your health, mind, and thought process. It is a good habit to interpret the data. The details provide in-depth information that will be useful in evaluating the exercise regimen.

IMPORTANCE OF AN EXERCISE BUDDY

There are occasions when you lose your motivation, and the regular workout becomes uninteresting. It will affect your morale and the commitment that you require to complete the regimen. If you are seeking a solution to improve your motivation and receive higher benefits from the exercise session, the workout buddy is the answer. In fact, possessing the exercise friend makes a lot of difference to the results. Although you may seem to conquer the activities all by yourself, having a friend by the side during the activities has its own benefits.

BENEFITS OF A WORKOUT BUDDY FOR KUSAL'S PROGRAM

1. Achieve fitness goals

With an exercise friend by the side, you will remain right on the track and receive the needed motivation throughout the activity. According to research by Stanford University, even a call from a friend every week helps in getting back on the track. You will work more and show higher output by the end of the week. The research showed that the result doubled within eighteen months. Having a workout buddy keeps you accountable and maintains the momentum necessary to move ahead with the regimen.

2. Fun

With an workout friend by your side, the tedious and routine of an exercise pattern becomes interesting and fun. It doesn't have to be serious. In fact, the results you achieve are directly proportional to fun you have. The more fun you have, the more you gain from the exercises. Working out alone becomes lonely and can have its disadvantages at times. Instead, with a friend by your side, you can laugh, share a joke, assist each other in an exercise, encourage, and motivate. Your exercise pattern never remains the same, and you would probably have a better time during the workout.

3. New activities

As they say, the numbers have power; you will probably find yourself in the best situation to try new workouts or patterns. You can have fun and be able to hit a CrossFit class or a session of yoga. The possibilities are endless, and every step brings you closer to your goal. At the same time, you will retain your confidence and develop it along the way.

4. Keeps you in the form

An interesting thing about having a workout friend is his/her ability to adapt to the role of the personal trainer. They can offer their assistance and help you achieve the right posture for any exercise. Even with little experience, they can offer their help in correcting the position. Remember, exercise is all about posture, control, and form. It helps you, especially when you switch over to new exercise patterns.

5. Competition

Many of us have a competitive streak. The presence of healthy competition gives us the ability to perform much better. According to a study, an individual performs enthusiastically when paired up with a fitter partner and motivation and morale are boosted. In another interesting finding, the participant worked 160% longer when paired up with a partner. It crossed the 200% mark when paired with an opposite sex. Man or woman, having a workout friend will help you perform better and achieve your goals with perfection.

6. Motivation

For many people, the presence of a partner adds motivation and strength to perform any activity. It makes an enormous difference and boosts the morale. You will enjoy the maximum support and motivation that you can ever imagine. You will be astonished to see your commitment towards the exercise regimen and reach your goals at a faster rate.

7. Check on ego

A workout friend helps you keep a check on the ego and keeps you grounded. Apart from encouraging, the buddy pushes you to do better without letting you get ahead of yourself. Check your ego at the door. Push yourself to be the best you can be. It's not a race. The benefits will ultimately help you.

8. Safe environment

Having an exercise buddy is beneficial when you choose strenuous exercises such as high resistance bench press or squats. The support they offer to the activity makes it a safe environment to perform it in the right way.

9. Variety

Your workout buddy will bring a different knowledge and skill set to the workouts. You will benefit from such variation and use it to the best while working out. They can introduce new variants and help you perform the activity with safety. A little variation in life adds to the fun and helps you avoid boredom.

10. Increase in commitment

Having an exercise buddy increases commitment. You will prepare for a schedule in advance. There is a possibility that you two will swap the workouts each time to try something new and interesting. Once you have the schedule on paper, it is likely that you will follow it with no excuses.

MONTHLY GOAL

Writing down a monthly goal helps in moving forwards with **determination and a plan.** Since, you already have an exercise friend, planning for the monthly goal becomes interesting.

You can share the goal with your partner and discuss the activities that you are planning to carry out. It helps in planning the schedule necessary for the 30-day period. You will probably have a lot going on in your mind. However, with the assistance of your partner, you can prepare a precise course of action that benefit in the end. Furthermore, make sure that the goal is something that you enjoy. Rather than develop a strict regimen, write it down in an interesting way that adds fun and excitement. For example, playing sport with the kids for two hours a day is more interesting to read than planning to lose five kilos. You will probably enjoy more when the goal relates and centers on everyday life. **You are bound to display enhanced passion and enthusiasm when you set goals that relate to your daily lives.**

With achievable and fun loving activity based goals, you are bound to enjoy every moment of it. Furthermore, the results are fascinating. You are bound to achieve the objective at a faster rate, and you may not even notice the progress. *The days pass by and very soon, it becomes a habit, making it an addition to your everyday life as a physical activity.*

YOU ACHIEVE YOUR SUCCESSES BY CELEBRATING YOUR SUCCESSES.

APPRECIATION DIARY

As exercise diary records your achievement and details about the training in detail, the appreciation diary helps to record memorable moments to your life. Write down five things at the end of the day that made you happy. Do not think about the challenges. All you have to concentrate on are the moments that made you happy, that you appreciate, that you have gratitude for. If you cannot think of anything because your world is full of 'things that are not going right for you' write down even the smallest things. For example, you might write down that you are grateful for a moment to breathe, a smile from a friend, or a song you like playing on the radio. You achieve your successes by celebrating your successes, no matter how small. Your successes flow when you look at life from a position of abundance.

Tracking the progress of the activity is an excellent method to promote motivation. The details help in understanding the development of the activity and the additional elements that can prove beneficial. You can measure the progress and check it every fortnight or every 21 days to differentiate the progress.

The addition of a new habit, every 21 days helps you to get on with the process of incorporating new things to your life. Evaluating the effect of the habit after 21 days provides you with the ability to check whether it has a significant impact. If not, you invariably have the option to revert back to normal life and find a new habit to introduce in your life. Life is all about learning and experiencing new things. The more you introduce, the more you learn and experience. It keeps you motivated and develops the self-confidence needed to overcome any challenge in life. Make sure that you add habits such as exercises, diet programs, quitting bad habits, and so on that have a positive impact on your life. Always find reasons that help you boost your motivation and self-confidence. Prepare a goal and divide into the small chunks. Make a schedule and reach the final goal in small steps. Take a moment to enjoy every step that you climb. It acts as self-appreciation and builds the needed positive attitude towards life. Share your moments with family and friends who always support you and your decisions.

Life is all about what you make. Make decisions that help you climb the steps of success. Reach the heights by scaling one-step at a time. Get on the journey and bring in number of people who would cheer for your success. Learn all the goodness in life and understand the purpose of your birth in life. When you do, you will have a clear visualization of the things that you have to furnish to scale the heights of success. You will be in a condition to lead a healthy and happy life.

21-DAY MEDITATION AND EXERCISE PROGRAM

WITH TIPS AND DETAILS FROM HELENE

PROGRAM INTRODUCTION:

Before opening my private practice in executive coaching, I worked as a researcher in a few different areas, including Preventive Cardiology, Positive Psychology, and Neuroscience. In my work in Preventive Cardiology, we were looking at the prevalence of morbid obesity in patients with major heart disease, type II diabetes and other life-threatening health concerns. In one study, part of my role was to work with patients who were extremely overweight to get them onto an eating plan that would support the improvement of their body mass index, or in other words, help them to lose weight. We had a team of incredible doctors and nutritionists on board, and I was learning from some of the best minds in the field. I recall a conversation with my boss, who was not only managing the project but was also a nutritionist herself, and we were discussing compliance concerns for the study. I was fairly new to patient care and management, and was not sure how to go about fulfilling my requirements in helping patients adhere to a rather strict diet plan, especially patients who had a history of pretty major food addictions. My boss told me to focus on helping our patients add in more good foods, rather than getting rid of bad foods. She also focused on making small changes rather than big ones. People tend to have a much easier time adding in more good things rather than depriving themselves of "bad" or destructive things, like food, alcohol, etc. Small changes are easier to integrate than big ones. With this in mind, our study was extremely successful. Our patients were eating more salads and less French Fries. Small changes were happening daily, and over the weeks in the study, significant weight loss and positive changes occurred. If we can take things just one step at a time, just one day at a time, and add in more good, healthy habits, we will start to see the old problems we faced naturally slip away, and the process just may be easier than you might think....

DAY 1

Theme of the day:
Permission

Tip of the day:
Give yourself permission to breathe

Exercise: 1 Deep Breath

Notes:
✓ Mindful
✓ Trying is doing
✓ Yes you can
✓ You just did it!

We always have the ability to take just 1 Deep Breath. No matter how busy our schedules, no matter how challenging our day, we always have this power. And when we begin with permission, permission from ourselves to ourselves, we are creating a positive line of communication within that will help us in ways that are as infinite as the human spirit.

Nourishment for the soul Tip/Recipe:
Hot Fresh Mint Tea

This is super easy. Simply boil some hot water, pour into a mug, add fresh mint leaves and let steep for 3 minutes. Enjoy a natural, caffeine-free antioxidant rich tea!

Today's 3-Minute EXERCISE

SHADOW BOXING

Directions: Elbows up, focus on the punch and push yourself to 85% intensity.

Description: Day 1 is all about getting started. When we give ourselves permission to breathe, we are opening the door to a tremendous world of positivity, love, support, care and nurture. When we give ourselves permission to take even one deep breath, we are taking an action step towards connecting with ourselves and our ability to care for ourselves in any moment, anywhere, any time.

DAY 2

Theme of the day:
Self-Care

Tip of the day:
Take a moment for yourself

Exercise: 2 Deep Breaths

Notes:

- ✓ Check in with yourself
- ✓ Slowly and surely
- ✓ One breath just like the other

Description: Day 2 is all about Self-Care. We are beginning a journey of taking care of ourselves from the inside out. When we do this, we are choosing to Feel Good, to Care For Ourselves, and to Be Solid For Those We Love. 2 Deep Breaths gives us a little more space to take a moment for ourselves. We expand our practice very slowly, taking baby steps along the way. It is in our courage to take even these small actions that we find our strength. We live each day one step at a time. We live our lives one breath at a time.

Nourishment for the soul Tip/Recipe:
Lemon/Lime Water

This is also extremely simple. Simply pour some filtered water into a glass or pitcher, add some fresh slices of lemon and lime, let sit out or in the fridge for about 5 minutes or more, and enjoy!

BONUS TIP: try to drink water before you are thirsty and stay hydrated throughout the day.

Today's 3-Minute EXERCISE

STAR JUMPS/JUMPING JACKS

Directions: Keep a straight spine, be upright and push yourself to 85% intensity.

DAY 3

Theme of the day:
Self- Love

Tip of the day:
Thank yourself for taking good care of you

Exercise: 3 Deep Breaths

Notes:
✓ Easy does it
✓ Slowly
✓ One just like the first and again
✓ You already know how to do this

Description: Day 3 is a beautiful day. Take a moment to congratulate yourself on taking the first 3 days towards a new healthy habit. The first 3 days are the most critical in creating a new pattern of behaviour. If you have come this far, you are setting yourself up for success with the rest. Just as build from Day 1 to Day 2 by adding 1 more Deep Breath, so we add another for Day 3. 3 Deep Breaths, though they may seem simple, are a full and complete meditation practice. It is in how we approach our breaths that determines how complete we feel with our practice. You have been breathing all of your life. You know how to do this. Perhaps there have been times when you felt your breath taken away such as a beautiful moment, a surprise, or an experience when time stood still. Even in these moments, our bodies have been breathing for us. In 3 Deep Breaths, we connect with our core expertise, our mind, bodies and spirits. In 3 Deep Breaths, we experience the truth of who we are.

Nourishment for the soul Tip/Recipe:
Dark Chocolate

For optimal health benefits, you will want to opt for 70% or more dark chocolate. A small square or two can boost immune system functioning, and offers a small dose of caffeine and calories to keep you going.

Today's 3-Minute EXERCISE

PUSH UPS

Directions: Maintain a straight spine and push yourself to 85% intensity.

DAY 4

Theme of the day:
Posture

Tip of the day:
Just like day 3, You Got This

Exercise: 3 Deep Breaths

Notes:

✓ Easy and gentle
✓ une into yourself
✓ Notice your center

Description: Practice makes perfect. When we hold ourselves in good posture, we align our bodies in a harmonious way. When we breathe deeply while aligned we open up good blood flow and circulation, and relax our muscles and minds in symphony. A practice of 3 Deep Breaths done with proper body position is much more effective in creating greater peace and clarity. I suggest sitting with nothing on your body crossed, palms resting facing upwards, and relaxing your shoulders and stomach. Take your inhales in through your nose, and exhale out through your mouth. This create a circuit of good clean air on the inhale coming in, and letting go of any stress or tension on the exhale, going out.

Nourishment for the soul Tip/Recipe:
Fresh Fruit

There are so many options when it comes to fresh fruit. Choose any that you like- apples, pears, grapes, grape fruits, berries, bananas- and enjoy any time of day. Eating smaller portions more frequently can help keep your energy levels up and your brain working at its best!

Today's 3-Minute EXERCISE

HIGH KNEE RUNNING

Directions: Keep your arms up and bring your knees to your hands each time. Push yourself to 85% intensity.

DAY 5

Theme of the day:
Core Connection

Tip of the day:
Rinse and Repeat

Exercise: 3 Deep Breaths

Notes:

✓ Notice the harmony from the Right to the Left, and Left to the Right sides of your body
✓ Keep it simple
✓ Gentle focus

Description: Day 5 is a great day to really get centered. When we breathe deeply, we are expanding our core on the inhale, breathing deeply into our diaphragms, expanding our lungs and opening up our chests. In this type of breathing, we are breathing into our very core, and on the mental level, opening up greater self-awareness. 3 Deep Breaths is a perfect amount to give ourselves a chance to Feel Our Center. As we deepen our meditation practice, feeling that connection with ourselves becomes easier and easier. Remember, this is a practice, not an art of perfectionism.

Nourishment for the soul Tip/Recipe:
Fresh Vegetables

Fresh Vegetables are a terrific option to keep your metabolism and brain functioning up. Any fresh vegetable can be a great snack at any time of day. When we focus on healthy options that we can add to our diets, as opposed to unhealthy items we need to subtract, we are setting ourselves up for a successful eating plan that supports our best health, weight and well-being.

Today's 3-Minute EXERCISE

CRUNCHES

 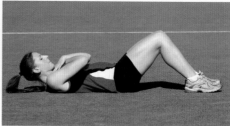

Directions: Push yourself to 85% intensity.

DAY 6

Theme of the day:
Slow and Slower

Tip of the day:
Practice makes perfect

Exercise: 3 Deep Breaths

Notes:

- ✓ Notice stress going out
- ✓ Notice good, clean energy coming in
- ✓ Notice yourself relaxing

Description: Now that we have 3 Deep Breaths going along rather easily, it is a great time to tune into the Speed of our breathing. Notice how long your inhale takes, notice the pause with the breath inside your body, and notice how long your exhale takes. Now, slow that down a little bit, and then a little bit more. Make each breath a bit slower than the last. Notice good clean energy coming in on those inhales, and notice any gunk or negative energy that you no longer need leaving you on those exhales, slowly and certainly. Make each breath an action of self-care. Make each breath an action of personal peace.

Nourishment for the soul Tip/Recipe:
Tea Tree Body Scrub

Taking a shower and using a tea tree body scrub can be a great way to awaken your senses while cleansing your body. Using an exfoliating scrub before adding the tea tree can open your pores up even more and increase the benefits. Breathe deep and enjoy!

Today's 3-Minute EXERCISE

SPINAL ROLL

Directions: Keep breathing with each movement. This exercise is all about achieving quality of movement.

DAY 7

Theme of the day:
You're Doing It Right!

Tip of the day: You are already doing it

Exercise: 3 Deep Breaths

Notes:

✓ Restful breathing
✓ Slow and steady
✓ Completing a
   week of self-care,
   I thank myself for
   my practice today

Description: "With These 3 Deep Breaths, I have completed my first week of my personal meditation practice, and for that I thank myself." Gratitude is the name of the game today folks. A full week of a dedicated practice is a big deal, and you have done Great! Today you are IN PRACTICE with your meditation. *When we acknowledge the good we do for ourselves, we reinforce those actions.* We can give ourselves positive reinforcement, because we deserve it. We earn it by showing up every day, trying a little bit more to be just a little bit better, fuller, more complete in who we are and who we are continuing to become. Today is a day to take stock and celebrate the success of a week of practice, growth, and commitment to yourself and your loved ones. With 3 Deep Breaths, we are choosing a path of awareness and growth.

Today's 3-Minute EXERCISE

TOWEL ROLL

Directions: The aim of this exercise is to relax on the towel. Do not push down on the towel, simply relax. Do not fall asleep on the towel otherwise you will cramp up.

1 Breakfast- Vegetarian Egg White Omelette with Fresh Fruit Salad

OMELETTE:

3 eggs
⅓ cup (80 ml) chopped fresh white onion
⅓ cup (80 ml) chopped fresh peppers
⅓ cup (80 ml) spinach
garlic
sea salt
black pepper
1 tbl. extra virgin olive oil

Directions: Heat up a medium sized skillet with olive oil, onions, peppers and spinach on medium heat. Add egg whites only, sprinkle garlic, salt and pepper to taste. Cook until egg whites are solid.

FRESH FRUIT SALAD:

½ apple
½ pear
10 green grapes
½ banana
3 strawberries

Directions: Cut all fruit into small, bite-sized pieces. Mix together and serve ½ cup with omelette. Makes 2 servings. Save one for a snack!

DAY 8

Theme of the day:
Slow and Steady

Tip of the day:
Choose Love

Exercise: 1 Full Minute of Breathing

Notes:

✓ Inhale: Good energy in
✓ Exhale: let go of anything that no longer serves you
✓ Slow and gentle

Description: Welcome to week 2. You have done a tremendous job getting here. You are now well on your way to creating a new healthy habit to support your best self. Peak performance happens with practice and commitment. Clarity, productivity and efficiency are like our muscles. They must be attended to often to gain strength and grow.

Today, choose Love. Love for yourself. Love for your practice. Love for your best performance. Love for your best self. Congratulations on being here, now.

Today's 3-Minute EXERCISE

CAT AND CAMEL

Directions: Feel each joint in the back stretching and moving gently. Focus on the quality of movement rather than quantity.

Nourishment for the soul Tip/Recipe:
Rebeca Rose Recipe
(on Instagram @rebecarose619)

Smoothie Talk

SMOOTHIES MUST HAVE INGREDIENTS

4 dates
½ banana
almond milk (Preferably your own almond milk and or almond butter or both)
½ apple (For extra liquid if you like it to be more sweet and juicy)
chia & oatmeal (dry or soaked)
cinnamon & Spirulina
fresh mint
½ pack of acai or berries of your choice
+ spinach, kale or chard
+ ice

These are my must have suggestions for making many different variety of smoothies to what you feel you need daily.

Switching up these ingredients and maybe adding a few more things you like can make so many different kinds of smoothie recipes. I like a variety! Some days I feel more juicy and other days I'd like more substance and something more filling. I mix up whatever I have or what I can get fresh at different local farmers markets. I find what I like and prefer to shop more often to get the best quality produce. It does take me time but nothing good ever came easy and the best things come in small doses I believe. Meaning I buy only little bits of things when I shop. I just have to make the effort to keep up and shop often, only getting what I need for a few days worth of food and buying what is fresh so my smoothies taste best!

DAY 9

Theme of the day:
It's all an experiment

Tip of the day:
Choose Health

Exercise: 1 Full Minute of Breathing

Notes:

✓ Inhale: Good energy in
✓ Exhale: let go of anything that no longer serves you
✓ Connect more fully with self

Description: We are stepping up our game! A full minute in full effect now. Take your time with this, noticing the good, clean energy coming in on those inhales. Notice yourself letting go of anything which no longer serves you going out with those exhales. One full minute of breathing is a beautiful place to be, and can really help you release any toxic energy you no longer need. When we breathe deeply, we connect more fully with ourselves. There are a number of new and exciting ideas here. For today, look at your practice as an experiment. Simply showing up, you have Won! We, with each breath, are choosing a practice to support our best health. In breathing deeply, we are connecting with a healthier, happier self. Today, choose to take a minute, a full minute, just for you.

Today's 3-Minute EXERCISE

WINDMILL ARMS

Directions: Start with larger circles and make them smaller over a 30 second period. Repeat going forwards and backwards until the 3 minutes are completed.

Eating Out

I LOVE TO GO OUT FOR PIZZA & PASTA.
But they're high calorie and full of carbs. Forget
the gluten free pasta and crusts. They're just as
high calories, carbs and starch. And, by the way,
rice flour has its own form of gluten.

So here's a tip for today.

Instead of pasta, ask for sautéed spinach and
broccoli. Ask them to sauté dry, so it's not watery.
Saves 300-500 calories and 50-150 grams of carbs.
You'll be happier at bedtime and in the morning.

Eating In

I LOVE SWEET POTATO FRIES! But boy are
they fattening. Forget the myth that they're so low
glycemic. They're not. A medium portion is over
400 calories and over 50 grams of carbs, 20 grams
of sugar. Here's a dish that will satisfy that itch.

Peel and slice eggplant about ⅛" thick. Cover
a baking dish with olive oil generously, and put
the eggplant on there, flipping a couple of times
so it's coated. Spray with baking spray and coarsely
ground salt. Put in a hot oven, 400°F, and turn
every few minutes, spraying and salting. It will get
brown and sizzle. Dry off a bit with paper towel and
serve. Sweet and salty, just like sweet potato fries.
Filling and Satisfying. You'll save 300-400 calories
per serving.

DAY 10

heme of the day:
Relax and Explore

Tip of the day:
Choose Clarity

Exercise: 1 Full Minute of Breathing

Notes:

✓ Inhale: Good energy in
✓ Exhale: let go of anything which no longer serves you
✓ Notice the balance in your body
✓ Notice your breathingsoftening

Description: We are now, officially, Rocking week 2! You are doing a tremendous job of showing up for yourself and integrating this new healthy habit into your day. If you have stumbled a bit, do not worry! *The path to success is rarely ever a straight line. Life is full of imperfections, and it is how we adjust and respond to the bumps along the way that define our successes and triumphs.* Today, our minute of deep breathing is dedicated to cultivating Clarity. In today's Meditation Minute, bring your awareness to the balance in your body. Take notice of the harmony within you. Soften your breath with each new inhale, and let go of anything which no longer serves you. Today is a day of relaxation and exploration. Enjoy your practice!

Today's 3-Minute EXERCISE

SQUAT JUMPS

Directions: Keep your back straight and push yourself to 85% intensity.

Nourishment for the soul Tip/Recipe:
Kitchen Sink Salad

Contributor: Chris Register, Founder and CEO of Brown Paper Los Angeles

"When our days at Brown Paper Los Angeles get hectic, our favorite quick and easy meal is a giant Kitchen Sink Salad that everyone can dig into. The massive bowlful of ingredients we have on hand usually includes up to eight elements: greenery, vegetables, protein, grains, fruit, fresh herbs, toppings, and dressing. You can easily adopt this method to throw together a light, healthy, filling meal almost instantly at home! Not only does this save you from thinking something up and turning on the oven, but it's also a fantastic way to use up all manner of random leftovers.

Salads sometimes get a bad rap for being "boring," but they don't have to be! With the right ingredients and a little creativity, salads can be visually stimulating flavor bombs that make you feel great about eating healthily. We recommend buying and using organic ingredients whenever possible, especially when produce is the star of a meal, for more vibrant, flavorful fruits and veggies in your salad. Adding a substantial amount of herbs is another great way to add tons of flavor and color to a dish without adding any additional calories, and you may benefit from their varied healing properties. Toppings like good quality cheeses or nuts are yet another wonderful way to add in some complex flavor and a little saltiness.

While flavor is important in any meal, so is its staying power. Beyond greens and veggies, adding some form of protein to a salad helps to make it more substantial, and will absolutely keep you feeling fuller longer. Grains also add some extra heft and protein to your salad, along with a satisfying chewiness that makes it feel like a full meal.

You'd be surprised at the myriad combinations you can toss together simply by hunting through your fridge, freezer, and pantry, but don't worry about how disparate your ingredients may be; dressing your salad helps to marry all of those different, yummy flavors together. When tossing your salad together, remember that delicate greens and thinly-sliced veggies prefer a light dressing, while more robust salads can easily stand up to equally robust dressings like buttermilk or green goddess.

GREENERY – Whether delicate like mesclun or hearty like kale, any kind of leafy vegetable works well as your salad's base. Don't be afraid to think outside the box and try some new ones, either, like lolla rossa, radicchio, or even shredded white and purple cabbage. It follows that mixing lettuce types, textures, and weights adds an extra element of interest and flavor to any salad.

VEGETABLES – Cubed, sliced, julienned, spiral cut, or shredded, use any combination of raw or cooked vegetables you like or have around. Cold or room temp works best, especially with more delicate greenery.

PROTEIN – Shred that extra chicken breast you grilled last night, rip up or cube deli turkey, or use up an awkward amount of leftover salmon. Vegetarians can simply drain and rinse a can of chickpeas or black beans, or use leftover baked seitan or tofu, or even some pre-cooked lentils.

GRAINS – Breath new life into that half-eaten take-out box of brown rice or Tupperware of leftover plain quinoa. Other grains like bulgur, faro, or even freekeh would also be delicious.

FRUIT – Small quantities of blueberries or strawberries, citrus like blood orange or grapefruit segments, or even diced mangoes add a hint of sweetness to salads. And don't forget everyone's favorite salad fruit, the avocado.

FRESH HERBS – Mint pairs magically with arugula, and romaine is enhanced beautifully by flat-leaf parsley or fresh tarragon. Fresh dill, chives, or even basil are all wonderful ideas too.

TOPPINGS – Parmesan, white cheddar, chevre, feta, pepitas, slivered almonds, sunflower seeds, or anything else with a salty bite!

DRESSING – a simple vinaigrette includes 3 parts oil (olive, grapeseed, etc.) to 1 part acid (citrus juice, vinegar, etc.), but our favorite go-to is a salty-sweet citrus dressing we use all the time. Try it with your Kitchen Sink Salad – and don't be afraid to tweak it based on what you've got on hand!"

DAY 11

Theme of the day:
Put yourself first

Tip of the day:
Choose Happiness

Exercise: 1.5 Full Minutes of Breathing

Notes:
✓ Just show up
✓ Slow and steady

Description: And today we up the ante again. As we move through our meditation practice cultivation process, these additions will set the stage for continued success long after the 21-day program. Today is about putting yourself first. As we take more time for our practice, we are taking more time for ourselves. No matter how busy your life is, no matter how hectic your day might seem, you have the power to take 1.5 minutes for You. Today is about choosing Happiness, choosing to do something for your greatest well being that will add to positive feelings and positive experiences. The big trick is not very tricky. The big trick is simply to Show Up. When we show up for our practice, we show up for ourselves. And remember, slow and steady.

Today's 3-Minute **EXERCISE**

PILATES ARMS

Directions: Keep the breathing consistent and the movements rhythmical. Do not push into pain. The quality rather than the quantity of movement is more important here.

1 Lunch- Spring Mix Salad with steamed tofu and balsamic vinaigrette

INGREDIENTS:

full bowl of spring mix greens
¼ cup (60 ml) sliced fresh peppers, thin
⅓ cup (80 ml) sliced fresh onion, thin
⅓ cup (80 ml) cucumber
⅓ cup (80 ml) shredded carrots
⅓ cup (80 ml) fresh avocado
1 tsp sunflower seeds
1 tsp dried cranberries
½ cup (120 ml) steamed tofu
¼ cup (60 ml) balsamic vinaigrette, any kind you like

Directions: simply combine all ingredients in a large bowl, toss to evenly disperse dressing, and enjoy!

DAY 12

Theme of the day:
Self-Love

Tip of the day:
Choose Joy

Exercise: 1.5 Full Minutes of Breathing

Notes:
✓ Just show up
✓ Slow and steady

Description: Most people do not think about Joy when they imagine a meditation practice. But why not? Meditation is all about connecting with the Goodness in Life. When we meditate, we are giving ourselves an opportunity to more fully feel the natural wellspring of joy already within us. Joy is an extension of love, light, kindness, compassion and care. Our meditation practice in and of itself is an act of self-love. As such, it is a door opener for us to feel that natural joy within, and a catalyst to share that joy with others. As we continue to show up For our practice, we may notice more joy showing up In our practice.

Nourishment for the soul Tip/Recipe:
Fresh Camomile Tea

Just like the fresh mint tea from day 1, this is a super simple recipe that will leave you feeling refreshed and rejuvenated. Simply boil some filtered water, pour into tea cup or mug, add some fresh camomile flowers, let steep for 5 minutes or more, and enjoy!

Today's 3-Minute EXERCISE

PILATES ARMS WITH SINGLE LEG UP

Directions: Keep the breathing consistent and the movements rhythmical. Do not push into pain. The quality rather than the quantity of movement is more important here.

DAY 13

Theme of the day: WIIFM-
What's In It For Me?

Tip of the day:
Choose Well-Being

Exercise: 1.5 Full Minutes
of Breathing

Notes:
✓ Just show up
✓ Slow and steady
✓ Listen and listen
some more

Description: It is Lucky 13 Day today, that's right, we are transforming the number into a lucky one! My dear friends at the Inspiration Campaign have decided to rule in favor of Good Luck with this number, and I say Yes! Today is about Choosing Well-Being. No matter what the mother-father-preacher-teacher tapes may tell you, no matter what the superstitions say, no matter what the haters and naysayers have told you, today is a lucky day. I encourage you to think about the WIIFM today, or What's In It For Me?

When we connect with WHY we are meditating, we are more likely to keep with our practice and have successful outcomes. Are you generally feeling more self-aware after you meditate? Has your stress level gone down after you breathe? Are you feeling more peaceful after you breathe? Are you finding a bit more mental clarity? Think about how your well-being is increasing as a result of your commitment to your practice, and thank yourself for showing up and listening to that voice within you who is telling you, Yes You Can.

Nourishment for the soul Tip/Recipe: Cucumber-Strawberry Water

Also a very simple recipe, simply pour some filtered water into a glass or pitcher, add fresh slices of cucumber and strawberry in equal parts, let sit for 5 minutes or more, and enjoy!

Today's 3-Minute EXERCISE

PILATES ARMS WITH BOTH LEGS UP

Directions: Keep the breathing consistent and the movements rhythmical. Do not push into pain. The quality rather than the quantity of movement is more important here.

DAY 14

Theme of the day:
Intention

Tip of the day:
Choose Peace

Exercise: 2 Full Minutes of Breathing

Notes:

✓ You are doing it right!
✓ Rest and relax
✓ Notice yourself relaxing more

Description: Welcome to the final day of Week 2! You are doing Great! Today we are taking our practice up to 2 full minutes. In today's breathing, I recommend starting by setting some intention. When we begin our practice by setting intention, we are setting ourselves up for a more present, more mindful practice. We have the ability to choose How we show up for our practice. Today I would like to suggest setting the intention of Choosing Peace. Peace, asThich Nhat Hanh puts it, Is Every Step. When we Choose Peace, we are choosing calmness, tranquillity, love and light. We are choosing the well being of ourselves and the well being of others. When we set the intention of Going Into Our Meditation Practice With Peace In Mind, we are opening the door to a Deeper Connection With The Peace Available Within Us In This And Every Moment. With each breath, you might notice yourself relaxing a bit more. With each breath, you might notice yourself resting and relaxing. With each breath, you might notice yourself experiencing more peace. Allow yourself to breathe in a groove, a flow, and set an intention that supports your greatest good, in alignment with the greatest good of all.

Today's 3-Minute EXERCISE

PILATES – DEAD BUG

Directions: You may only be able to do this exercise for 15-20 seconds when you start, that's ok. It's all about control and quality of movement, that's what makes it hard.

1 Dinner- Veggie-crumble stir-fry with brown rice and mixed vegetables

INGREDIENTS:

1 package veggie crumble (morningstar, boca)
½ cup (120 ml) water chestnuts
½ cup (120 ml) fresh peppers
½ cup (120 ml) kale
½ cup (120 ml) spinach
½ cup (120 ml) whole kernel yellow corn
⅓ cup (80 ml) shelled edamame
1 tbl. sesame oil
1 tbl. extra virgin olive oil
3 tbl. Bragg's amino acids
garlic powder
sea salt
cayenne pepper
paprika
black pepper
2 cups (475 ml) brown rice

Directions: Cook rice separately in a large pot with plenty of space for rice to cook and expand. Add spices and some oil to taste if desired.

In a large sized skillet, add oil and veggie ground first. Sauté on medium heat, adding various vegetables slowly and mixing together as you go. Add Bragg's amino acids and spices once all ingredients added. Turn heat to simmer and cook for 10-15 minutes, stirring occasionally. Serve over rice and enjoy!

DAY 15

heme of the day: Clarity

Tip of the day: A healthy mind is a perfect partner to a healthy body

Exercise: 2 Full Minutes of Breathing

Notes:

✓ Relax into it
✓ Notice the increased peacefulness in your mind

Description: Welcome to Week 3!! You have not arrived in the home stretch of integrating a New Healthy Habit! Congratulations, you have achieved something that many never do in an entire lifetime! Again, if you have had some bumps along the way, that is quite alright. Be gentle with yourself, and just keep trying. If you are one of the few who have been able to stick to a daily practice every day for the past 2 full weeks, please do take a moment to acknowledge your consistency. As of today, consistency is crucial. If you have not already done so, pick a time on your calendar where it is convenient for you to take a few minutes to breath and set a daily reminder. Try to stick to the same time every day. If pausing during your regular day is too risky, I recommend breathing in the shower or in bed before going to sleep. 2 minutes is all you need today. As you breathe, notice the clarity of mind that

Today's 3-Minute EXERCISE

PILATES – FOUR POINT KNEEL WITH LEG EXTENSIONS

Directions: Keep the spine straight and maintain this as the leg extends out.

comes with the continued breathing. Notice how it makes your body feel. A healthy body and healthy mind are perfect partners. As you support your practice and your mental clarity, you just may see your body transforming in positive ways. Our muscles relax, our jaws unclench, our shoulders open, our stomachs calm, our brains register the good we are doing for ourselves and our bodies benefit with each and every breath.

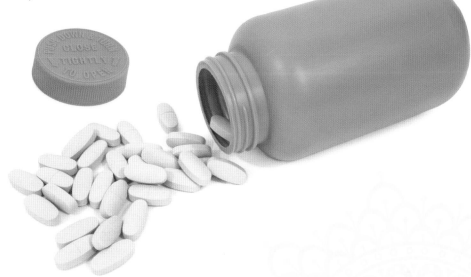

Nourishment for the soul Tip/Recipe:
Multi-Vitamins

Go for a plant-based vitamin if you can. If you have any specific needs, look for higher concentrations of things like Iron or B Vitamins if desired. The trick here is to Be Consistent. Getting into a habit of 1 multi-vitamin each morning with breakfast can help boost overall health and well-being, immune system functioning, brain functioning, and keep you feeling energized.

DAY 16

Theme of the day:
Balance

Tip of the day: A little self-care goes a long way

Exercise: 2 Full Minutes of Breathing

Notes:
✓ Slow and steady
✓ Show up and listen
✓ Notice yourself slowing down

Description: Today's meditation is dedicated to internal balance. Balance is very simply the state of being in harmony. As we breathe, we might notice the harmony from the right to the left, and the left to right sides of our bodies. We might notice how our minds relax with each breath and a greater sense of mental balance is more readily experienced. We might have thoughts come up, but keep breathing and feel that balance and harmony despite any disturbances. When we approach our practice with the mentality that 'a little self-care goes a long way' we are capable of being in the moment. We do not need to perfect our life-long meditation skills. We do not need to be perfect even in today's practice. All we need to do is show up. That's it. That's all it is. No, really. Just show up and breathe. And as we breathe, you will feel yourself slowing down, tuning in, and feeling a little bit more balanced, a little bit more harmonious. If you experience any surges of stress, breathe and let them go. And then keep breathing. Breathe for yourself, and breathe nice and slow.

Nourishment for the soul Tip/Recipe:
Acidophilus

Acidophilus is one of many probiotics, which help us break down our food and aid in digestive health. Getting into the habit of taking 1 probiotic, such as acidophilus each day can help us keep our intestinal tract clear and clean. Taking a probiotic when eating starchy carbs or sugars can help our bodies digest these foods more efficiently. A clean body supports a healthy mind.

Today's 3-Minute EXERCISE

PILATES – KNEEL AND LEAN

Directions: Keep the spine straight and do not let the hips drop onto your knees as you move backwards.

DAY 17

heme of the day:
Less Is More

Tip of the day: Little by little, I feel better every day

Exercise: 2.5 Full Minutes of Breathing

Notes:

✓ Resting,
  I breathe in
✓ Resting,
  I breathe out

Description: Day 17 and we are going Strong! Fantastic job in getting this far! You are getting very close to a fully integrated practice. At this point you may find that it is getting easier to show up and breathe. Let's stretch just a little bit more today and go for 2.5 minutes. Yes, you can. In today's meditation I encourage you to think about keeping it simple. *Less is more.* All we are doing is breathing. As we breathe, we rest. A simple mantra may be "Resting, I breathe in. Resting, I breathe out." With each

breath, we are shifting from a state of disconnect to connection. We are choosing to let go of that which no longer serves us. We are connecting with the love and light within, and allowing that love and light to flow through us with each breath, sharing that energy with those in our lives simply by Being. You may

Today's 3-Minute EXERCISE

GLUTEAL STRETCH

Directions: This is a stretch so do each leg for 30 seconds. Repeat 3 times and then swap sides. Remember to keep breathing through the stretch.

notice that each day of your practice now feels a little better than the last. At this point, your neurophysiology is likely actively supporting this new healthy habit. As our neuroplasticity takes effect, our brains begin to wire In Support Of This Habit. The more we can connect with How Good It Feels to breath and check in with ourselves, the more physiological support we will have. Keep it simple today, breathe, and feel good. Enjoy your practice, and love your day.

Nourishment for the soul Tip/Recipe: Vitamin C

There are all kinds of ways for us to keep our immune system happy and active. Vitamin C is one of the most researched and effective ways to do this. 1,000 mg of Vitamin C each day can support an increase in immune system functioning, as well as an increase in energy and feelings of vitality. It is best to break this up into 2 500 mg doses for optimal absorption.

DAY 18

Theme of the day:
Keep It Simple

Tip of the day: Practice
leads to Peacefulness

Exercise: 2.5 Full Minutes
of Breathing

Notes:

✓ I trust myself to be
  healing towards
  myself
✓ I am showing
  up for my own
  healing journey

Description: Welcome to
Day 18. Generally, when we
think about this number in
terms of years of age, this is
the age when people become
an adult by legal standards
here in the USA. 18 is a rite
of passage in a way. Similarly,
18 has significance in many
spiritual practices and groups.
There is a milestone here. As
we practice, we are walking the
path towards greater peacefulness. And along the way,
we are acting in a way that is
healing towards ourselves. As

we act in a way that is healing
for ourselves, we are in essence
showing up more fully for our
own healing journey. We have
all lived lives filled with joys
and challenges. Our world is
filled with opportunities to
learn about how strong we are,
sometimes through triumphs
and sometimes through
painful experiences. In our
healing journey, a meditation
practice can offer solace and
support in any moment, in
any place, at any time. As we
continue to show up consistently for our practice, we
are allowing greater healing
to take place for our minds,

bodies and spirits. When we
keep it simple, we are connecting with the simplicity of
love. When we keep it simple,
we are connecting with
the simplicity of peace. When
we keep it simple, we are
connecting with the simplicity
of our spirits. And in that
simplicity, we just may be
able to catch a glimpse of
the infinite nature of the soul.
It is in the simplicity that we
know the infinite, and in the
infinite that we experience all
that is simple. In each breath,
we are showing up for who we
are in the moment, and that is
a beautiful practice.

Today's 3-Minute EXERCISE

SUBSCAPULARIS SHOULDER STRETCH

Directions: This is a stretch so do each arm for
30 seconds. Repeat 3 times and then swap sides.
Remember to keep breathing through the stretch.

Sweet Oven Fried Eggplant

INGREDIENTS

2 large eggplants
olive oil (medium grade, like from Costco
or any inexpensive private label brand)
coarse salt (I like Himalyan Pink Salt in
a grinder, but you can use any coarse salt)
PAM® or other baking oil spray
aluminum foil
a large baking sheet
a cutting Board and sharp butcher's knife
a plate and paper towel.

1. Preheat Oven to 400°F. Convection Setting is best

2. Cut the top and bottom off the Eggplant and peel it so there's no skin left (I recommend you DON'T leave the skin because it will separate and make the dish more bitter and harder to eat)

3. Rinse the Eggplant in fresh water

4. Cut the Eggplant lengthwise once or twice, depending on size. You will be making slices about 1 ½" wide by 3" long, ideally.

5. Slice the Eggplant in about ⅛" thick slices. Too thin, it will burn, too thick, it will be mealy and less sweet.

6. Cover baking sheet with aluminum foil (when I was a kid we called it "Tin Foil". Odd, eh?)

7. Pour olive oil on the covered baking sheet. There should be enough oil so that the eggplant slices don't float but can be moved around easily. Better to use a little too much oil than too little, unless you like the Eggplant dark brown and crispy.

8. Swish slices around a little, and turn them over. They should be flat on the sheet.

9. Spray slices well with oven spray.

Grind salt over the slices. If you like really salty, use more. Remember, the right kind of salt can make things a little sweet. That's why I like Pink Salt. Also, fresh coarse ground salt has less "sting" and a little more sweetness.

10. Put them in the oven.

11. The first 5 minutes they get hot, and soft.

12. Turn them when they start to brown. Spray the other side and salt.

13. Keep turning and spraying every 2 minutes until all the eggplant is bubbly, and gets a brown coating.

14. Some of the pieces will be very brown and a little crispy, others will be softer. You decide what you like better. You may want to take some out in the midst if your oven is uneven, like most of our ovens.

15. Dry on paper towel and put in a bowl, just like the fries. The sweetness means you can "86" the ketchup.

16. Congrats. You've indulged and saved yourself 400 calories. Yes, it's got oil, but so do the Fries. And there's almost no sugar…and no need for ketchup. And a really LOW glycemic index. It takes some doing, but so does going to the gym."

DAY 19

Theme of the day:
Permission

Tip of the day: I give myself permission to take time and energy to support my best self

Exercise: 3 Full Minutes of Breathing

Notes:

✓ Resting,
  I breathe in
✓ Resting,
  I breathe out

Description: Today is a graduation day. We are graduating to a full 3 minutes of breathing. This is your next chapter. Should you remain with this practice for the rest of your life, you have everything you really need. Of course there is more, but you will find it within if you do not pursue it externally. Today, we give ourselves Permission to step into a full 3 minutes practice. Today, we are allowing ourselves to take even more time to connect with our harmony, our peacefulness, our state of flow. Today we are giving ourselves permission to take this 3 minutes of time and energy to support our best selves. Again, we might use the simple mantra, "Resting, I breathe in. Resting, I breathe out." And with each breath, another step towards your greatest well being is taken. With each breath, another step towards the he or she you came here to be is achieved. With each breath, another moment of truth and connection is experienced.

Today's 3-Minute EXERCISE

HIP FLEXOR STRETCH

Directions: This is a stretch so do each leg for 30 seconds. Repeat 3 times and then swap sides. Remember to keep breathing through the stretch.

Contributor: Chris Register, Founder and CEO, BPLA

BPLA's Rice Wine Vinegar and Lime Dressing

INGREDIENTS

¼ cup (60 ml) rice wine vinegar

4 tsp agave

2 tsp dijon mustard

2 tsp minced garlic

2 tsp freshly squeezed lime juice

¼ cup (60 ml) extra virgin olive oil
(or grapeseed oil)

any extra fresh herbs you might want to use
kosher salt and freshly ground black pepper
to taste

Directions: The easiest way to make this vinaigrette is to toss everything into a mason jar, seal it with a lid, and shake vigorously until all ingredients are smooth and incorporated. (You may also store the vinaigrette in that sealed jar for about a week in the fridge.) Alternatively, whisk together the rice wine vinegar, agave, mustard, garlic, and lime juice in a large mixing bowl. Continue whisking as you slowly drizzle in the oil, until all the ingredients come together. Season with salt and pepper to taste. Enjoy!

DAY 20

Theme of the day:
Self-Care

Tip of the day: Supporting my best self supports those around me

Exercise: 3 Full Minutes of Breathing

Notes:

✓ Resting,
   I breathe in
✓ Resting,
   I breathe out
✓ I am listening

Description: Self-Care is like black suits in New York City, it's always in style. They style of the suit, however, matters, as does the style of self care. If we push too hard too fast, we might actually stress ourselves out and fall out of fashion. So the question is, how can we find our own personal perfect style? Is it possible to find a meditation style that fits me as perfectly as my favorite suit, sweater, or even those old jeans that no matter how many holes they have I will never throw away? Of course a meditation practice can be customized and stylized! Day 20 is a great time to start thinking about what might make my meditation practice even better. With 3 minutes of deep breathing every day, I am showing up for my daily self-care ritual. When I do this, I am not only supporting my best self, but also supporting those in my life, because when I am at my best, everyone benefits. So in our practices, we can show up, we can breathe, we can listen to that inner voice. We can ask ourselves, what else would I love in my customized

Today's 3-Minute **EXERCISE**

ARM SWINGS

Directions: Push yourself to 85% intensity.

meditation practice? Am I in the best environment for my practice when I breathe? Do I have the right clothes on? Am I in the sunshine or inside? Today, simply breathe, and allow yourself to think about what you would most love as your meditation journey continues….

Nourishment for the soul Tip/Recipe:
Green Tea for Energy

There are lots of options when it comes to an energy boost. Green tea has a small amount of caffeine and high amounts of antioxidants. One small cup of green tea can boost brain functioning and metabolism, and can give us a bit more energy to tackle our day!

DAY 20 IS A GREAT TIME TO START THINKING ABOUT WHAT MIGHT MAKE MY MEDITATION PRACTICE EVEN BETTER.

DAY 21

Theme of the day:
Self-Love

Tip of the day:
Supporting my best self supports the greater good

Exercise: 3 Full Minutes of Breathing

Notes:

✓ I choose love
✓ Resting,
   I breathe in
✓ Resting,
   I breathe out
✓ I choose peace

Description: Today is a day of Victory! With these 3 minutes, you have completed a full 3 week cycle of integrating a new healthy habit, beginning a daily meditation practice, and cultivating

Today's 3-Minute EXERCISE

PALM TREE

Directions: Hold the posture for 15-60 seconds. It will be tough at first but keep repeating it for the full 3 minutes.

a commitment with yourself to be loving to You! Self-Love is one of the most essential skills we can cultivate in our lives. There will Always be plenty of people who will have lots of "great ideas" about who we 'should' be, and how we 'should' spend our precious time and energy. And yet, our lives are not about pleasing everyone else all the time. Our lives are about finding out what truly feels right for ourselves, and in that space of connection with self, understanding our part of the global family. When we support our own best self, we are by extension and connection supporting the greater good. We live in this world Together. We breathe in this world Together. We Love in this world Together. Let us help one another to find that sense of peace, harmony, love and light with each breath. As we care for ourselves, we are caring for all.

Nourishment for the soul Tip/Recipe:
Whole Wheat Penne Recipe

Delicious Waistline-Friendly Pasta

INGREDIENTS:

1 lb. whole wheat penne
⅓ cup (80 ml) extra virgin olive oil
¼ cup (60 ml) crushed garlic
⅓ cup (80 ml) fresh basil leaves
1 whole fresh red pepper, cut into thin slices
1 small white onion, cut into thin slices
1 cup (240 ml) cherry tomatoes, cut in halves
2 cups (475 ml) fresh broccoli florets
black pepper
sea salt

Directions: In a large pot, cook penne to desired firmness, drain and let sit aside. Sautee all other ingredients in large pan separately on medium-low heat for about 5 minutes. Add in the penne, toss and enjoy! Sprinkle parmesan or fresh cilantro on top for additional flavor.

DAY 22

Where do we go from here?

You have achieved something that many people never do. A consistent daily meditation practice is no small thing. You are setting yourself up for tremendous opportunities for positive thinking, positive experience, positive connection and positive meditative journeys. You have already done the hardest part, getting your practice started! Keep going! Stay with the 3 minutes exercise, and when you feel you have mastered that step, pick up our next book for the next chapter of your journey to begin.

Congratulations on what you have accomplished. When you increase your well-being, the whole world benefits. Thank you for your practice.

CHAPTER 6

TIPS FOR GUARANTEED SUCCESS

Although we are busy in our daily life, we spend the same energy every day to perform various activities. "I wish I had more time" and "I couldn't achieve this because I ran out of time" are standard excuses that come out a lot. When you think about it, the most successful out there have the same amount of time as you and I. So how do they make it happen? The problem lies within ourselves. Lack of motivation, your drive and how much you believe in yourself are other reasons that influence your day and productivity. The following tips provide you an opportunity to succeed in your daily life and build the needed confidence to move ahead without hesitation.

5 KEY TIPS FOR SUCCESS FROM KUSAL

1. Prioritize

It is significant for you to prioritize the activities of the day. Time management plays an influential role in how you perform several activities in a day. If you have the ability to perform several tasks within the stipulated time, you do not have to worry about anything, as you possess the needed confidence to complete all your work. However, if you do not, then it is time for you to prepare a schedule where you arrange your activities according to their priorities'. You have to consider each task as an impact to your productivity and growth. You can achieve success at the end of the day when you carry this out as scheduled. Continuing to work on your tasks that are 'important' rather than 'urgent' will bring you closer to your long-term goals.

2. Pay attention

Paying attention is crucial in regards of the amount of work to be completed. Many successful people pay detailed attention even to smaller things. You will probably move ahead without turning back, by paying attention to finer details. It emphasizes that the work is perfect. If you perform your duties with concentration and on time, you will leave nothing behind. You will learn to judge every work in the right way and avoid errors along the path. As it becomes a habit, you will improve everything in your life and the way you lead it.

3. Efficient and effective - difference

Learn the different between efficiency and effectiveness. Both are equally important for you to scale the ladder of success. It's necessary to learn how you can be effective and efficient. The path defines your success at any work that you handle. Learning this ability will give you the power to control several activities in a smart way. All you have to do is find activities that create an effect in an efficient manner, which assists you in scaling the success steps.

4. Positive attitude

Positive thinking has an impact on every action that you carry out. It will take you a long way and takes you on a life-journey that you never experienced before. Make sure to fill your mind with positive energy. Meet people who talk positively. Join clubs that encourage and boost morale. You can even gain confidence and remain confident when you complete a task on time. Set a goal and divide it into small chunks. Rise slowly towards the goal by completing the smaller fragments. At the same instance,

it is imperative that you shield against all the negativity. Keep away from people who you think are a hurdle to your success.

5. Solve big problems

Problems come in different sizes and shapes. You should be in a situation to differentiate them and place them in the right category. Learn to solve problems that are challenging and rewarding. Furthermore, professional and personal problems are sometimes intertwined, with each one's effect closely affecting the other. Most will fear their biggest problems and give up and there is no way that you will reach your goal. You have to solve the biggest problem that is ahead of you to move forward. Solving the biggest problem will align your smaller problems therefore allowing you to tackle these in an easier fashion. It is the only way that you can cross this path and reap benefits.

GOAL SETTING

Many people work hard but do not seem to climb the ladder of success. You may be one among them. The primary aspect of this situation is because you have not set a target in your life. You are still confused about the things that you want from life. Every person has a destination they may want to reach. Its imperative to work out where you want to get to. After all, you would not set on a long journey without any destination, probably not. Right?

Setting targets or goals are essential because you will motivate yourself to move towards that target. You will set schedules and have a clear picture of the things that you want. With better understanding of the goal and the requirement,

you will head towards with a specific action that will help you reach the destination.

By possessing knowledge of where you want to go in your life, you will able to plan the course with precision. You will receive the answers you need to all your questions that concentrate on your weaknesses. You will further avoid unwanted circumstances or hurdles that might pull you down from climbing the success ladder.

STARTING

Begin with the bigger picture of what you want from your life. Identify the goals that you want to achieve to reach the final destination. Once you identify, break the goals into smaller chunks so that you can easily reach them without much stress and energy. Once you have the vision, it is time for you to prepare the steps necessary to achieve the smaller goals.

"THE FOLLOWING IS THE PROCESS THAT WILL HELP YOU PREPARE OR SET UP YOUR GOAL IN LIFE AND MEASURE IT CONTINUOUSLY THROUGHOUT TO ENSURE THAT YOU ARE PROGRESSING TOWARDS SUCCESS."

– KUSAL

Step 1: Initial setup

The first step consists of initiating the process to set up the goal. It is the primary asset to the entire program. Seclude yourself from the rest of the world for a few hours and think about what you want to do in your life. Consider all the aspects, your passion, your activities so far and interests to ensure that you will receive the answer to your question. Set the goal for your life but not for a short period. Setting long-term goals gives you a clear perspective on the things that you require for moving ahead with the program. Always make time for yourself to do this. It will help bring perspective to your goals, how you may need to achieve their success and other brilliant ideas that are delving deep in your subconscious mind.

Give the balance to the goal by considering your career, financial status, education, family, attitude, physical status, pleasure, and public service. Spend time to brainstorm about all the categories and their effect on your goal. The session enables you to come up with different objectives in each category. You can then pick a relevant goal or step that adds to the final target of your life. In the end, make sure that the goals that you have set are the ones that you want to achieve. Do not consider the likings or feelings of others such as parents, family members, or friends. It should be yours and yours alone.

Step 2: Smaller goals

After you have setup the lifetime goal, divide the goal into equal lengths such as a three-year plan or smaller goals. These smaller goals play a crucial role in helping you move towards your lifetime goal.

Go further and divide the three-year plan to one-year or a six-month plan. You can then equally prepare a monthly progress card for each goal. It will give you a better idea about the things that you have to do to climb every step one at a time. Every plan uses the previous as the foundation. You will then have to create a To-Do list. The To-Do list assists you preparing the things that you have to complete and reach the one-month target. The smaller goals will be simple in the beginning and gradually increase as you gain confidence. Such an approach helps you in improving the quality of life and provides you with a better understanding of your destination.

Review your plan and check whether all the activities included run towards your vision. The plan will give you the chance to change based on the input that you have selected. You perpetually have the choice to change the plan if you sense that the action plan is not exactly that you imagined. However, ensure that you do not overburden yourself.

Step 3: Staying on course

After you have prepared the daily To-Do list, you have to ensure that you follow the plan without missing a beat. Every time something is completed in your To-Do list, enjoy the moment by crossing it off the list. Enjoy the mini-celebrations as you go. Set a day where you evaluate the progress. Keep the evaluation day short. For example, set a 21-day deadline for the measurement. According to research, the mind requires 21-days to create a new habit and accustom to it.

With the help of the details in the diary, you will check the level of your progress. You can even further check whether you are heading in the right path. You can ask your partner or confidante to review the course. The second-person's involvement can keep you alert and ensures that you move on the right way.

SMART GOALS

SMART goals are those, which are measurable. You will only progress when you can measure the previous sessions or past days productivity. SMART stands for Specific, Measurable, Attainable, Relevant, and Time-bound. For example, you can set a goal, as "I have to lose five kilos in another five months". It is a concrete and measurable goal that is also attainable, relevant, and time-bound.

Step 4: Additional tips

Setting goals and preparation for the same is useful in moving towards your vision. The following offer you additional tips during your preparation for setting the goals:

✤ Make sure that every statement that you write is positive. Express your goals as positive statements.

✤ Make your goals precise and to-the-point. Come up with a deadline for the goal and put in the dates. It is the easiest way to measure the progress. You can even analyze the details and make changes for the following day to improve the plan. You can even check whether you are on the right track or drifting away.

✤ As you have set several goals, prioritizing each one is imperative. Priorities help you achieve the goal in a systematic approach. You will attain confidence and the energy that assists you in moving ahead.

✤ Write down the goals on paper. Look at them every day. Check your progress at the beginning, during and at the end of the day.

✤ Keep the operational steps small. If a step is too large, then you will make slow progress. Keeping the steps small and attainable makes sense. This allows you to easily complete the to do list in an enthusiastic way. As you are moving towards the things that you like to do, it will be fun and exciting. Celebrate this.

✤ Performance goals have the upper hand over outcome goals. Check your performance but not the results of the goal. The performance will be your skills, thought process, motivation levels, self-confidence, and the way to look at challenges. When you can measure them and see the difference, you will quickly scale the heights without any trouble.

Step 5: Taking a moment

After the achievement of a goal with success, take a moment to celebrate and enjoy the result. Take the time to savor the first step towards your destination. It builds satisfaction, motivation and enhances inner strength. Include your family members and friends who helped you through the stage. Or simply take moment to sit silently, celebrate your achievement, smile and bathe yourself in the pleasure of your smallest of achievements.

Alongside the success, measure and review the progress of other set goals. Make sure that the goal that you achieved is not too easy. If it is easy, ensure that the next goal pushes you outside your comfort zone. Consider the time taken to reach the goal. If the next goal is long, prepare it in such a way that you consume it in reduced time. If you have gained new knowledge that is helpful in moving towards your vision, keep this in your repertoire, you will be able to use it with ease in the future. If you sense a deficit of a particular skill, despite the success, decide whether fixing this will influence your life.

Taking a moment to enjoy the success. This helps in successful progress towards your destination. Take the time off and evaluate, compare, add, and delete a few things from the rest of the goals based on the current victory. Do not rest with a single win. You have a long journey ahead and time does not stop for you. Make sure that you move along with time and as planned according to the schedule.

Use online tools to track and monitor the progress of your goal. Apart from keeping a diary to record, the online apps help you analyze a number of options. The spreadsheets will calculate the tedious procedures and revert with answers.

KEY POINTS

Setting a goal is of immense importance. Heading life without understanding your contribution is unrealistic. Every person has a role to play in this world. People who understood this mere fact scaled the ladder of success.

MAKE SURE THAT THE GOAL THAT YOU ACHIEVED IS NOT TOO EASY.

Of course, there are sacrifices, but you will reach the point where each sacrifice is a step closer to where you want to get to. Learn to understand the importance of your life in this world. Prepare a life vision that you really want to do and make progress. Separate yourself from unwanted things and concentrate on the factors/elements that help you move ahead towards your destination. Take a moment to enjoy success at every interval. It increases your self-confidence, boosts morale and builds the strength necessary to overcome any challenge that you might face in the future. Involve people who think positively and move forwards with your like minded team.

Here's the first thing you should do now that you have finished: Thank yourself!!

You might want to fill this out at the start of your program so that you can look forward to your reward. Simply fill in the blank:

My reward to myself is _____ .

THESE ARE HELENE FINIZIO'S TIPS TO GUARANTEE SUCCESS AND WHAT TO DO ON A DAILY BASIS

A. Use Peak Performance Mindset Thinking (PPMT) Daily

1. The best way to do it, is to do it! Take a few moments to check in with yourself and your thinking, and if your thoughts are not fully supporting you, change them! You have this ability any time, any day, any where.
2. The key ingredients for PPMT
    a. Hope
    b. Optimism
    c. Future-Mindedness

B. Take Your Time

We need not rush the process. If we are showing up and doing our best, we are already succeeding. Our culture focuses on getting things done yesterday, but all we really need to do is show up in the here and now.

C. Keep It Simple

Just 1 deep breath when done mindfully will a practice make. We do not necessarily need to do a lot, we just need to be present for what we choose to do.

Less Is More. We are busy people with busy lives. If we can keep our self-care routines simple, we are much more likely to have successful outcomes and positive experiences.

D. Consistency is Key

Healthy habits come from integrating new routines. This comes from practice, time and patience. If you can, commit to yourself every day. Show up for your practice and it will become a new habit that you find yourself going to more automatically before you know it!

E. Thank yourself for your practice

Gratitude is one of the most powerful forces in the Universe. When we practice gratitude, we are acknowledging ourselves for the good we are doing, and acknowledging the good all around us. Gratitude at the end of a meditation practice also closes out the meditation space itself, allowing our minds to shift more easily back into "normal" mode.

F. Reward yourself for your practice

Positive reinforcement can be up to five times more effective than negative reinforcement in securing new patterns of behaviour. We can use this to our advantage and employ positive reinforcement to integrate positive habits such as meditation and exercise all along the way. It is also another way to practice self-care and self-love.

G. Don't rush the process

There is a maxim I often use with my clients, and that is: "Never too far too fast." Our natural tendency is often to rush the process, when we never need to. The baby steps Are the journey, and it is a beautiful thing when we can relax and enjoy the scenery along the way.

H. Be gentle with yourself

Being gentle with yourself is perhaps a little easier to say than to do. We all tend to be our own worst critics. Very simply put, this is all about Being Your Own Best Friend. If you can keep this in mind, you will be practicing self-care As you develop your meditation and mindset practices, as well as your exercise practice. The exercises themselves can be experienced as difficult or as easy, it is all about how you approach them.

I. Don't leave it up to memory

This is the #1 problem I see in my private practice in executive coaching. Busy people tend to carry a lot of information in their minds all day long. A new habit will easily get lost in the shuffle if it is not scheduled just like any important appointment or meeting. I recommend setting a reminder on your calendar. Choose a time that works for you every day and you will likely find a much easier path to a successful outcome.

J. Choose Your Words Wisely

"Words do not label things already there. Words are like the knife carver: They free the idea, the thing, from the general formlessness of the outside. As a man speaks, not only is his language in a state of birth, but also the very thing about which he is talking."
– Intuit Wisdom

When we practice mindful speaking, it asks us to show up with greater integrity through and through. Our meditation practice can help us tune into ourselves and know what really feels like our truth. As we practice positive thinking styles, we might find more confidence to speak authentically and with less filtering. If we can show up and speak our truth mindfully, we are allowing others to really get to know who we are, and allowing ourselves to create a life that truly feels right for us.

The most important conversation for creating new healthy habits is the conversation we have with ourselves. Be true to yourself.

Daniel Khaneman of Harvard University studied the nature of long-term memory storage of various types of events such as colonoscopy procedures. He and his team found that people tended to rate their experience based on the peak moment of the procedure, perhaps the moment of greatest sensation, and the end. In this particular study, they found that people who had the probe left inside one's body without uncomfortable motion at the end of the procedure were much more likely to return for a follow up procedure than those who wrapped up just as motion stopped, feeling more discomfort right at the end. The results of this and other studies led Khaneman to develop the Peak-End Theory, in which he states that we form long-term assessments of experiences based on the peak and end of an experience. Therefore, if we have a very pleasurable experience at the peak of a vacation, for example, but a very bumpy flight home, then overall we may remember the trip as less enjoyable than if we had had a smooth flight. What this means is that the end of an experience is very important in our desire and willingness to do something again. When we reward ourselves, we are supporting more positive integration of long-term memory access of an experience, such as starting a new exercise routine or meditation practice. Reward yourself, and even the more difficult moments will seem easier each time you try again.

HERE ARE SOME ASSESSMENT TOOLS FOR MASTERY

a. Consistency measurements- did you complete the exercise every day for 21 days?

b. Time completion- did you finish the full time suggested?

c. Bonus points for: insights and AHA moments recorded (unanticipated benefits)

You might want to keep a journal handy and record any insights and AHA moments along the way.

d. 1-10 ratings daily on (1 being the least and 10 being the most)

i. Peacefulness

ii. Clarity

iii. Stress

iv. Productivity

v. Efficiency

vi. Happiness

vii. Well being

viii. Concentration

ix. Optimism

x. Positive self talk

xi. Quality of sleep

What are some positive outcomes and benefits you can expect from a consistent daily practice of meditation and PPMT?

a. Get into the moment before a performance

b. Better sleep/rest/relaxation

c. Happier with mind and body

d. Increased concentration

e. Increased self-awareness

f. Better connection with self

g. Increased optimism

h. Increased exercise

i. Increased healthy habits

j. Increased healthy thinking styles

From the Authors

Life is what you make of it. It is in our power to create the life we would most love to live. A positive attitude is our own responsibility, and can be a gift that we give to ourselves. Knowing that this is in our own hands, we can select the processes we want and need to turn our lives into something healthy, happy and joyful each and every day. When you choose a positive attitude, you are just by example helping others to choose the same, and can more actively help others on their path in life as well. Go ahead! Move forward with that positive energy, that determination, that motivation and that active mind of yours! Make a choice to improve the quality of your own life, your own health, and you will be helping not only yourself, but the people you love as well. You have the power to create your best day, Every Day. You already have everything you need, and you always will. Trust yourself, and make it happen.

All our best,

Kusal and Helene

INDEX